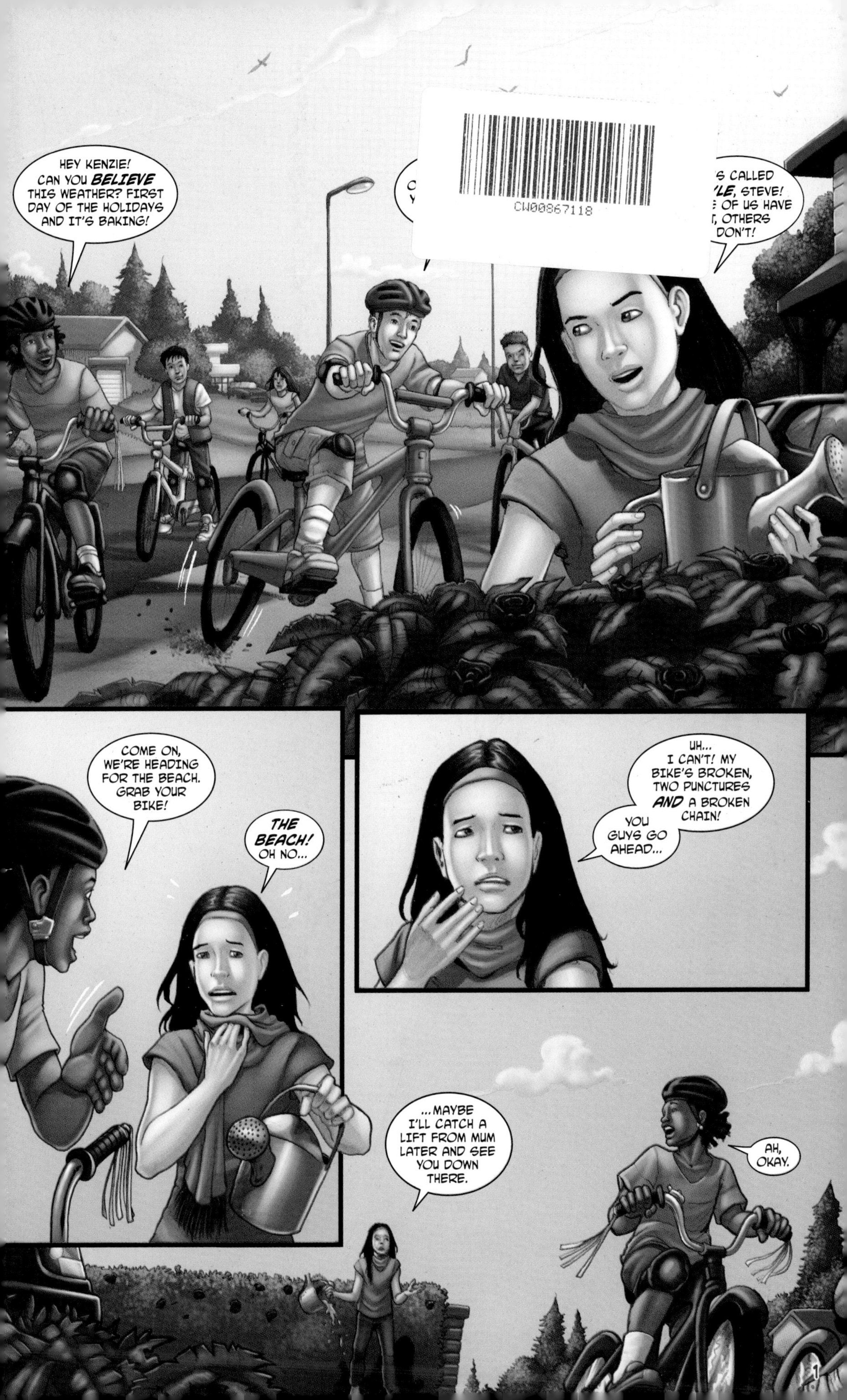
HEY KENZIE! CAN YOU BELIEVE THIS WEATHER? FIRST DAY OF THE HOLIDAYS AND IT'S BAKING!
COME ON, WE'RE HEADING FOR THE BEACH. GRAB YOUR BIKE!
THE BEACH! OH NO...
UH... I CAN'T! MY BIKE'S BROKEN, TWO PUNCTURES AND A BROKEN CHAIN!
YOU GUYS GO AHEAD...
...MAYBE I'LL CATCH A LIFT FROM MUM LATER AND SEE YOU DOWN THERE.
AH, OKAY.

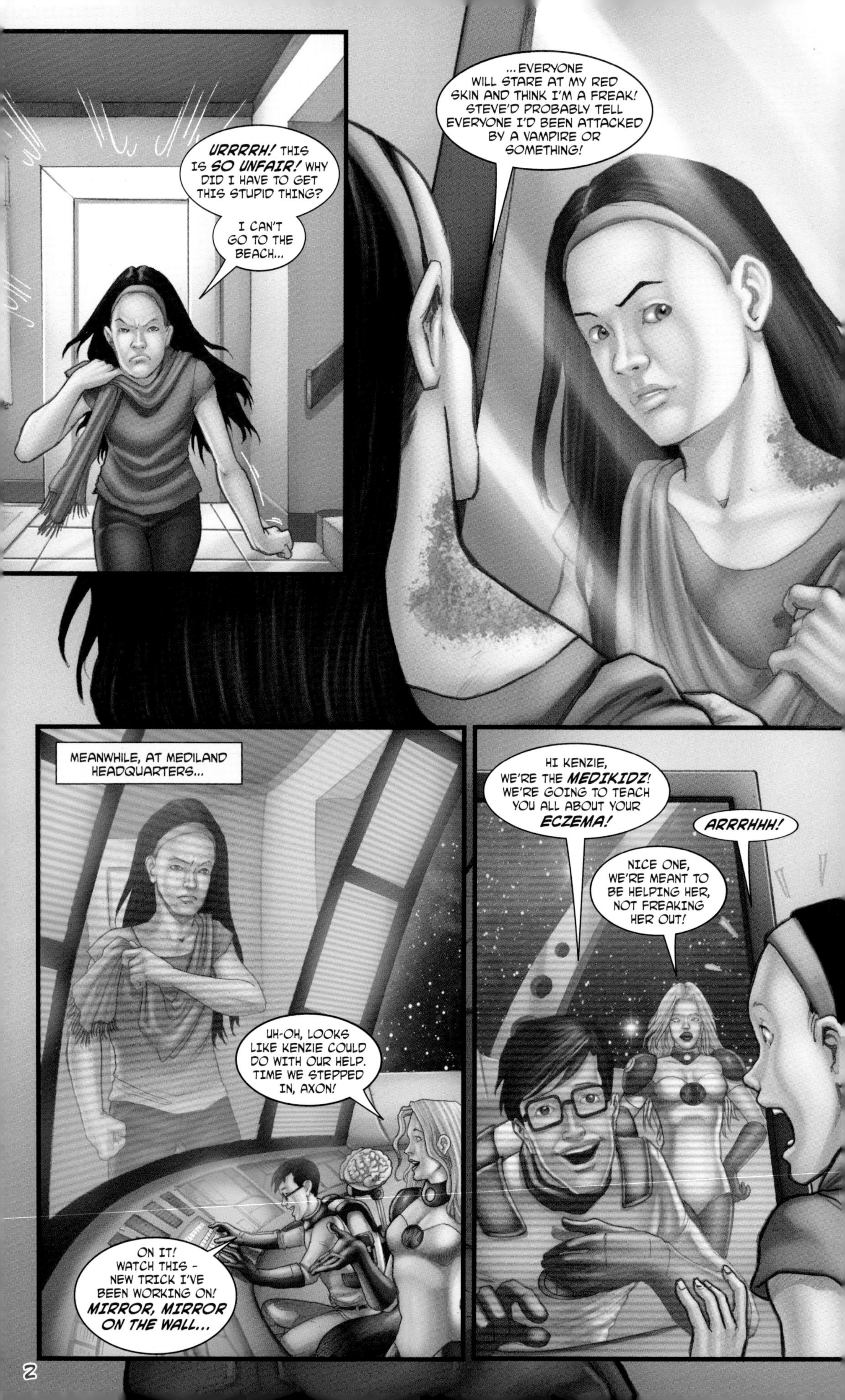
URRRRH! THIS IS SO UNFAIR! WHY DID I HAVE TO GET THIS STUPID THING?
I CAN'T GO TO THE BEACH...
...EVERYONE WILL STARE AT MY RED SKIN AND THINK I'M A FREAK! STEVE'D PROBABLY TELL EVERYONE I'D BEEN ATTACKED BY A VAMPIRE OR SOMETHING!
MEANWHILE, AT MEDILAND HEADQUARTERS...
UH-OH, LOOKS LIKE KENZIE COULD DO WITH OUR HELP. TIME WE STEPPED IN, AXON!
ON IT! WATCH THIS - NEW TRICK I'VE BEEN WORKING ON! MIRROR, MIRROR ON THE WALL...
HI KENZIE, WE'RE THE MEDIKIDZ! WE'RE GOING TO TEACH YOU ALL ABOUT YOUR ECZEMA!
ARRRHHH!
NICE ONE, WE'RE MEANT TO BE HELPING HER, NOT FREAKING HER OUT!

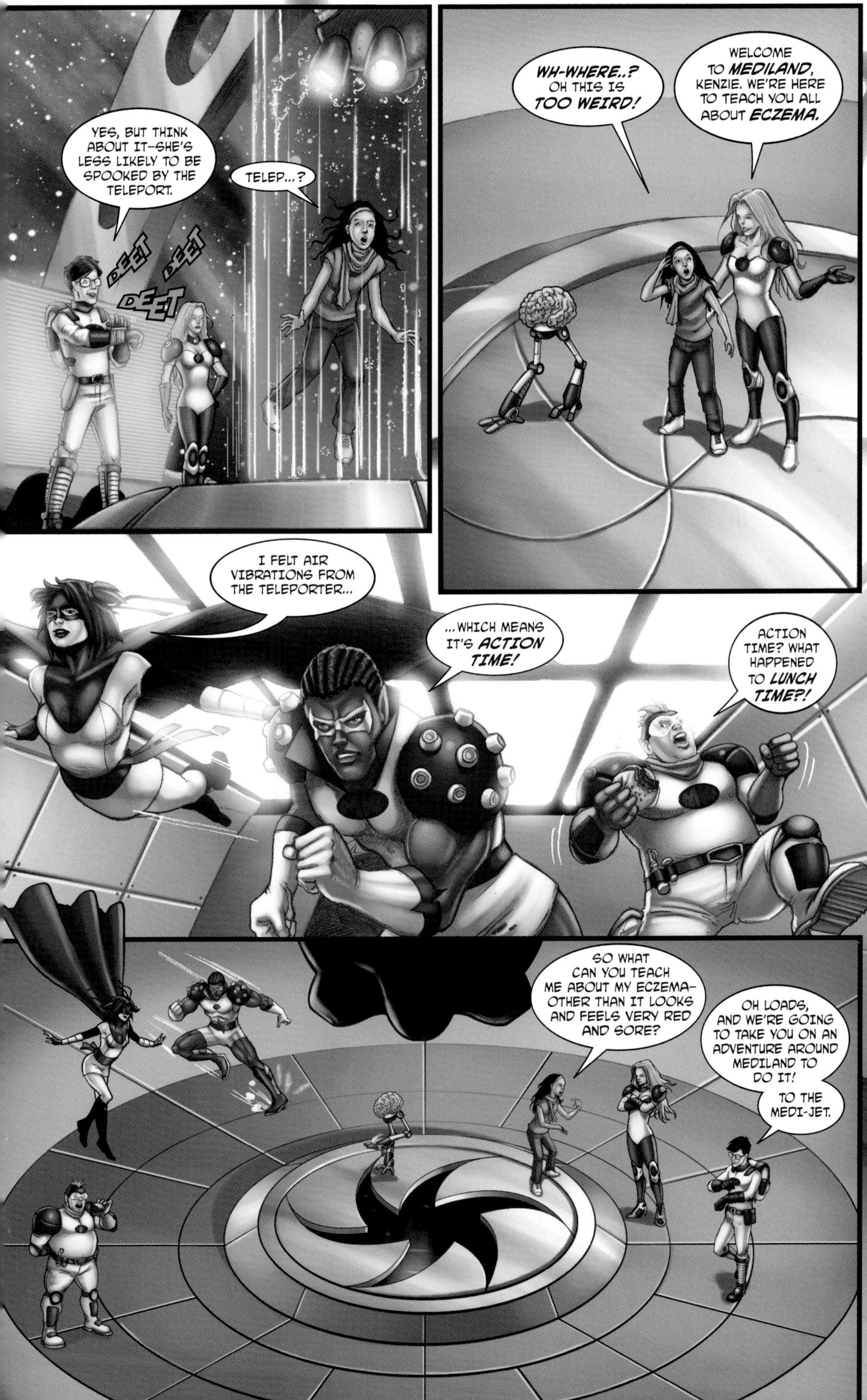
YES, BUT THINK ABOUT IT–SHE'S LESS LIKELY TO BE SPOOKED BY THE TELEPORT.
TELEP...?
DEET
DEET
DEET
WH-WHERE..? OH THIS IS TOO WEIRD!
WELCOME TO MEDILAND, KENZIE. WE'RE HERE TO TEACH YOU ALL ABOUT ECZEMA.
I FELT AIR VIBRATIONS FROM THE TELEPORTER...
...WHICH MEANS IT'S ACTION TIME!
ACTION TIME? WHAT HAPPENED TO LUNCH TIME?!
SO WHAT CAN YOU TEACH ME ABOUT MY ECZEMA– OTHER THAN IT LOOKS AND FEELS VERY RED AND SORE?
OH LOADS, AND WE'RE GOING TO TAKE YOU ON AN ADVENTURE AROUND MEDILAND TO DO IT!
TO THE MEDI-JET.

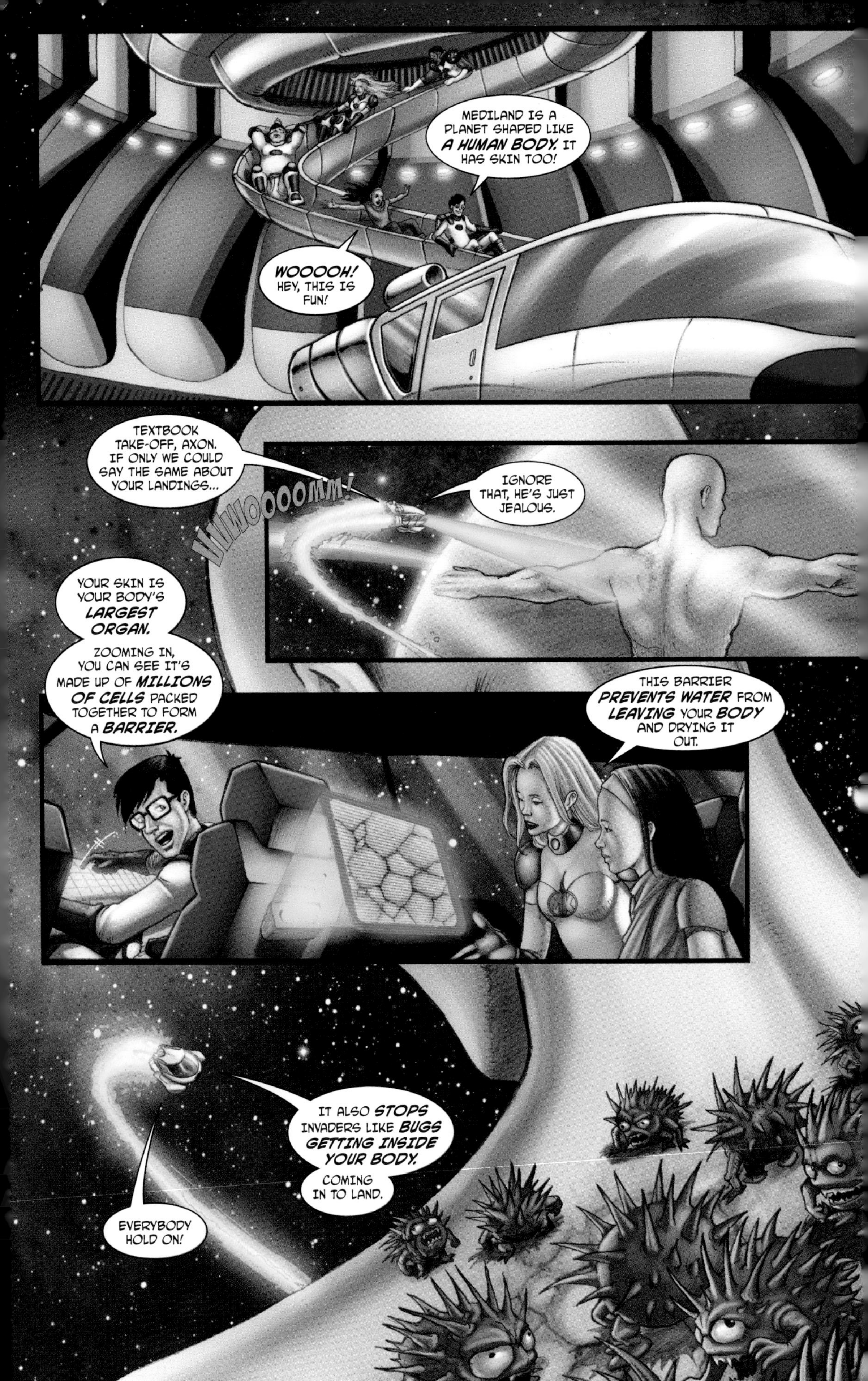
MEDILAND IS A PLANET SHAPED LIKE A HUMAN BODY. IT HAS SKIN TOO!
WOOOOH! HEY, THIS IS FUN!
TEXTBOOK TAKE-OFF, AXON. IF ONLY WE COULD SAY THE SAME ABOUT YOUR LANDINGS...
VVVWOOOOMM!
IGNORE THAT, HE'S JUST JEALOUS.
YOUR SKIN IS YOUR BODY'S LARGEST ORGAN.
ZOOMING IN, YOU CAN SEE IT'S MADE UP OF MILLIONS OF CELLS PACKED TOGETHER TO FORM A BARRIER.
THIS BARRIER PREVENTS WATER FROM LEAVING YOUR BODY AND DRYING IT OUT.
IT ALSO STOPS INVADERS LIKE BUGS GETTING INSIDE YOUR BODY.
COMING IN TO LAND.
EVERYBODY HOLD ON!

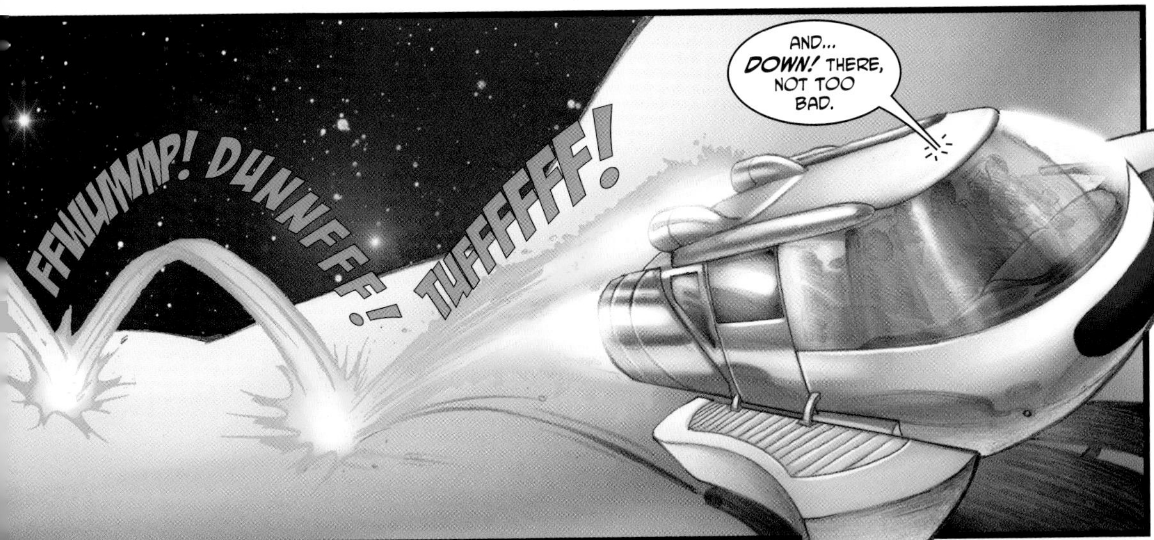
FFWUMMP! DUNNFFF! TUFFFFF!
AND... DOWN! THERE, NOT TOO BAD.

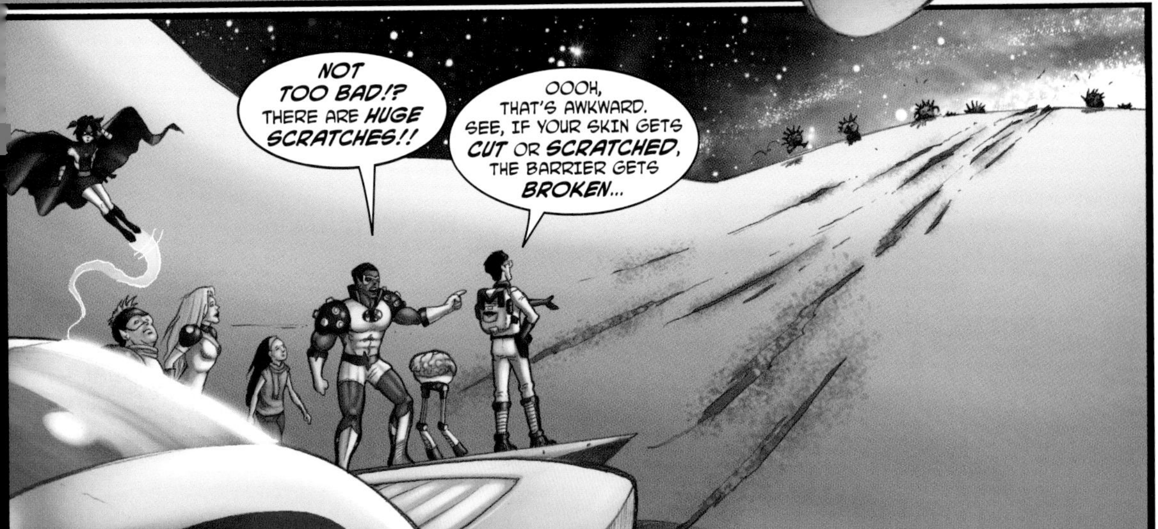
NOT TOO BAD!? THERE ARE HUGE SCRATCHES!!
OOOH, THAT'S AWKWARD. SEE, IF YOUR SKIN GETS CUT OR SCRATCHED, THE BARRIER GETS BROKEN...

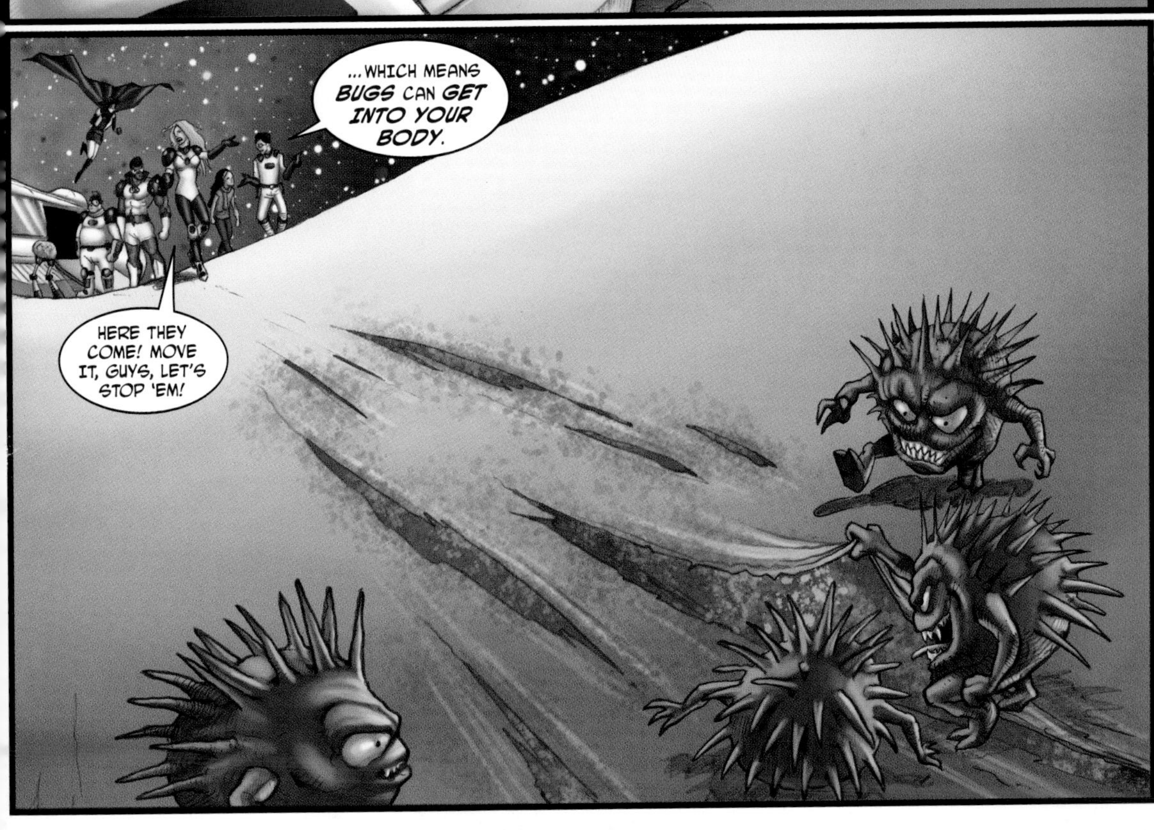
...WHICH MEANS BUGS CAN GET INTO YOUR BODY.
HERE THEY COME! MOVE IT, GUYS, LET'S STOP 'EM!

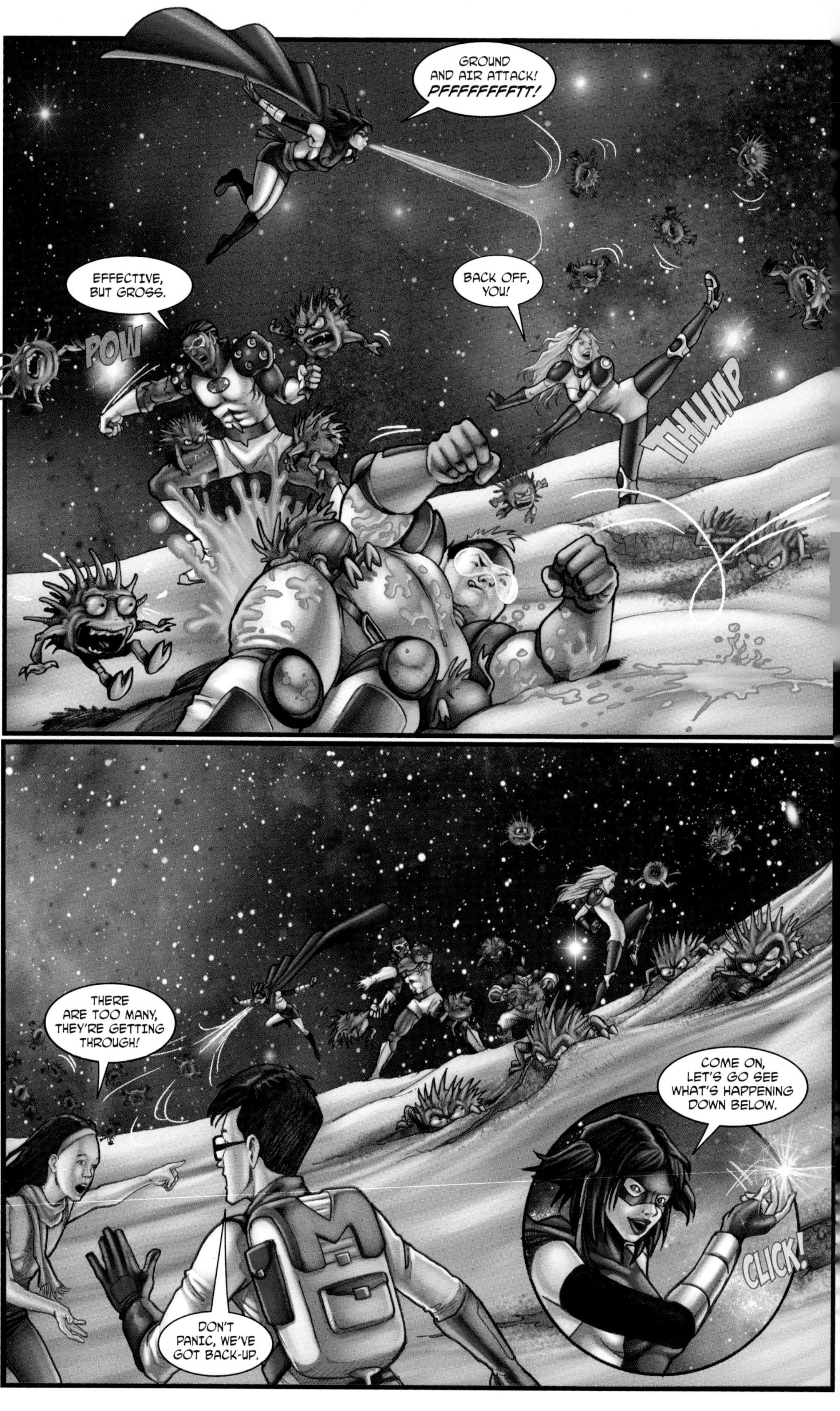
GROUND AND AIR ATTACK! *PFFFFFFFFFTT!*
EFFECTIVE, BUT GROSS.
POW
BACK OFF, YOU!
THUMP
THERE ARE TOO MANY, THEY'RE GETTING THROUGH!
DON'T PANIC, WE'VE GOT BACK-UP.
COME ON, LET'S GO SEE WHAT'S HAPPENING DOWN BELOW.
CLICK!

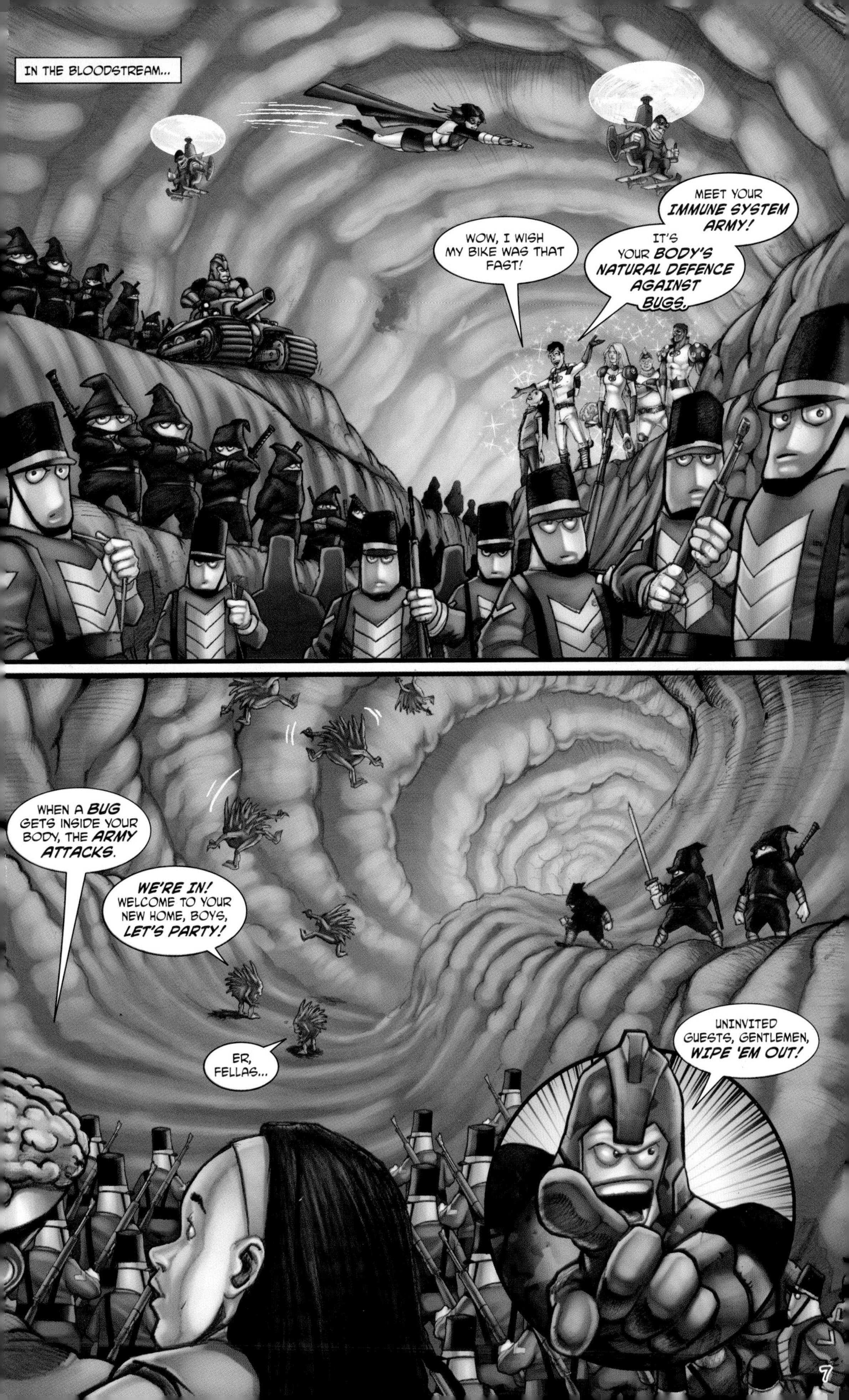
IN THE BLOODSTREAM...
WOW, I WISH MY BIKE WAS THAT FAST!
MEET YOUR IMMUNE SYSTEM ARMY!
IT'S YOUR BODY'S NATURAL DEFENCE AGAINST BUGS.
WHEN A BUG GETS INSIDE YOUR BODY, THE ARMY ATTACKS.
WE'RE IN! WELCOME TO YOUR NEW HOME, BOYS, LET'S PARTY!
ER, FELLAS...
UNINVITED GUESTS, GENTLEMEN, WIPE 'EM OUT!

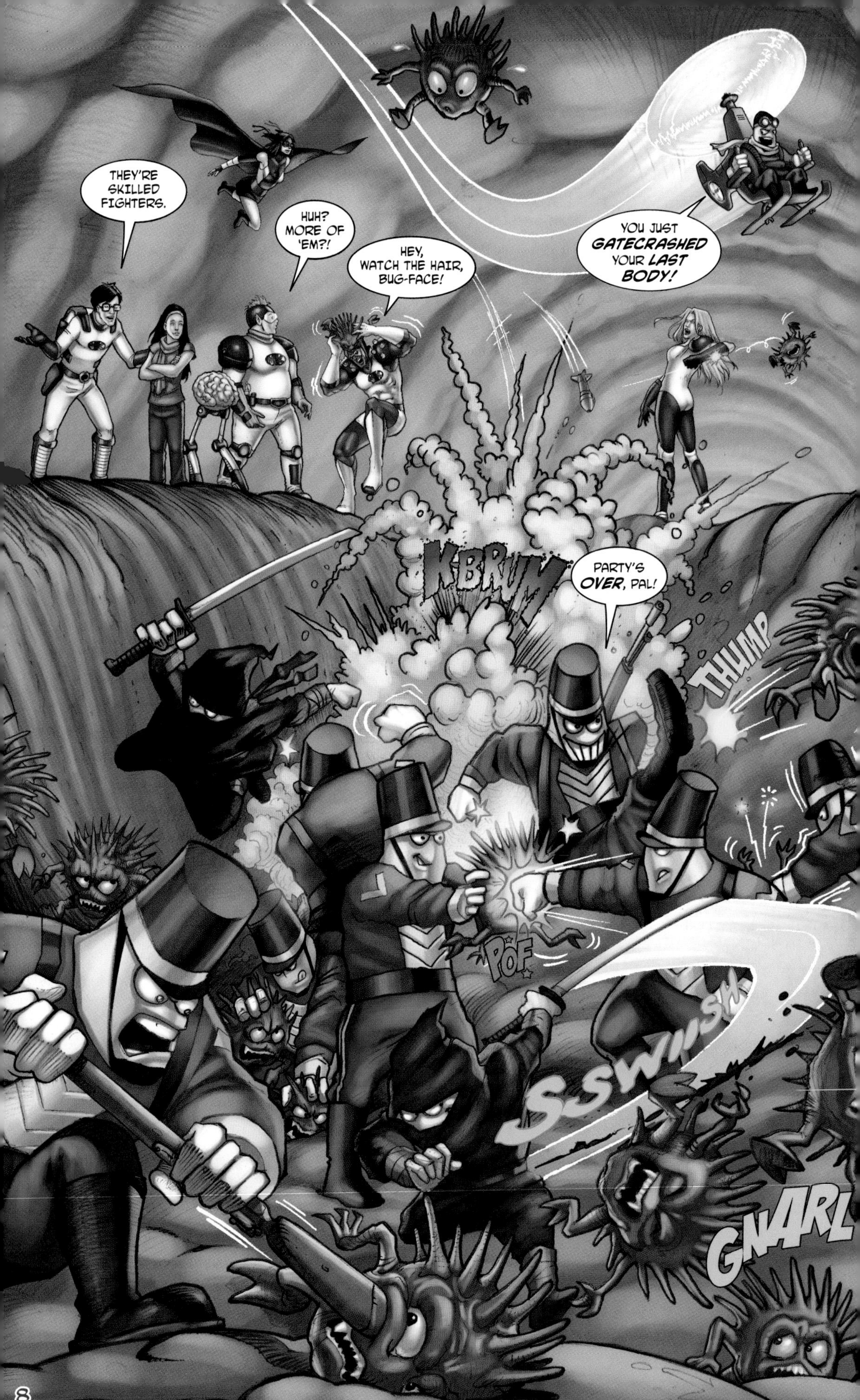
THEY'RE SKILLED FIGHTERS.
HUH? MORE OF 'EM?!
HEY, WATCH THE HAIR, BUG-FACE!
YOU JUST GATECRASHED YOUR LAST BODY!
KBRUM
PARTY'S OVER, PAL!
THUMP
POF
SSWISH
GNARL

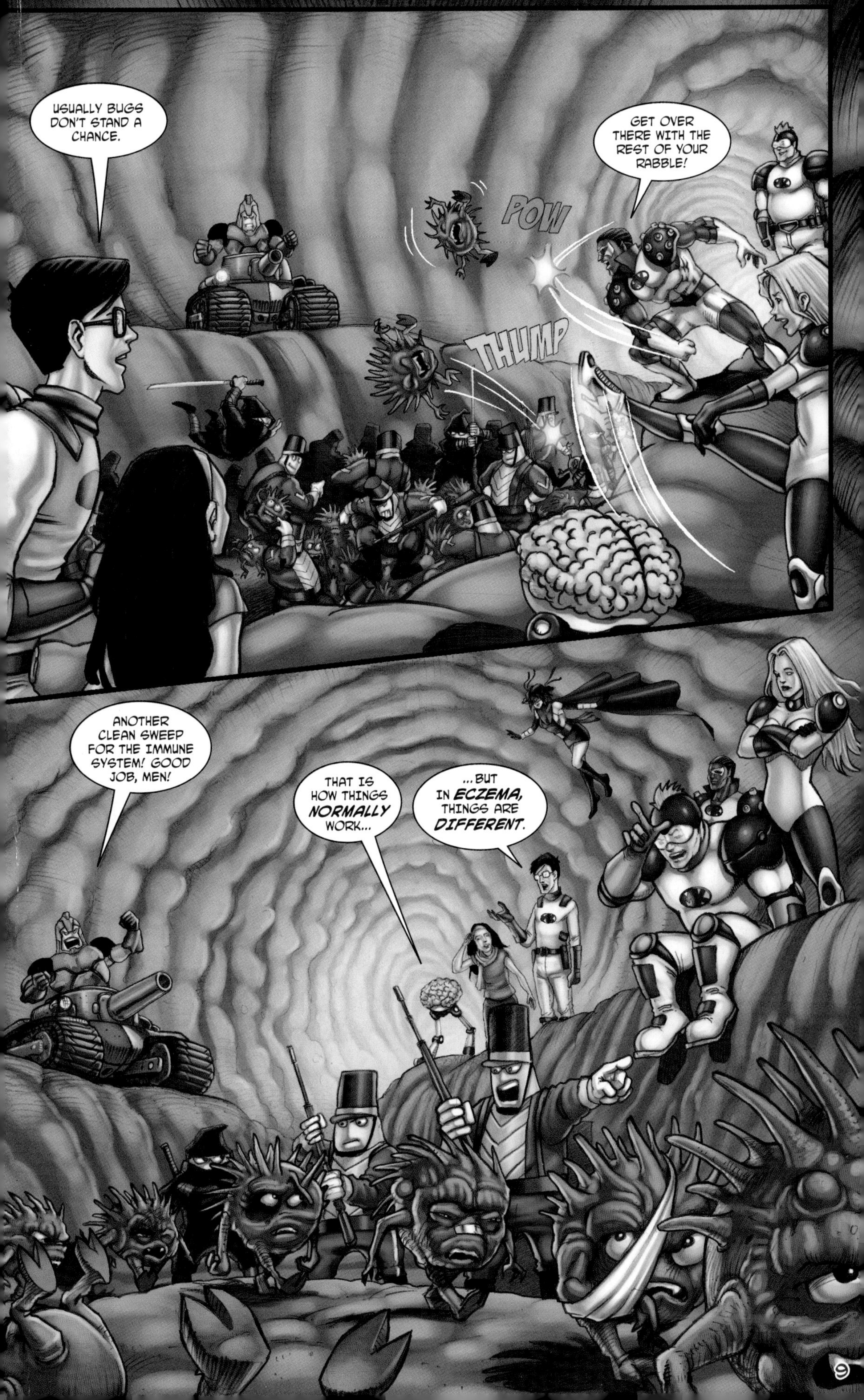

USUALLY BUGS DON'T STAND A CHANCE.
GET OVER THERE WITH THE REST OF YOUR RABBLE!
POW
THUMP
ANOTHER CLEAN SWEEP FOR THE IMMUNE SYSTEM! GOOD JOB, MEN!
THAT IS HOW THINGS *NORMALLY* WORK...
...BUT IN *ECZEMA,* THINGS ARE *DIFFERENT*.

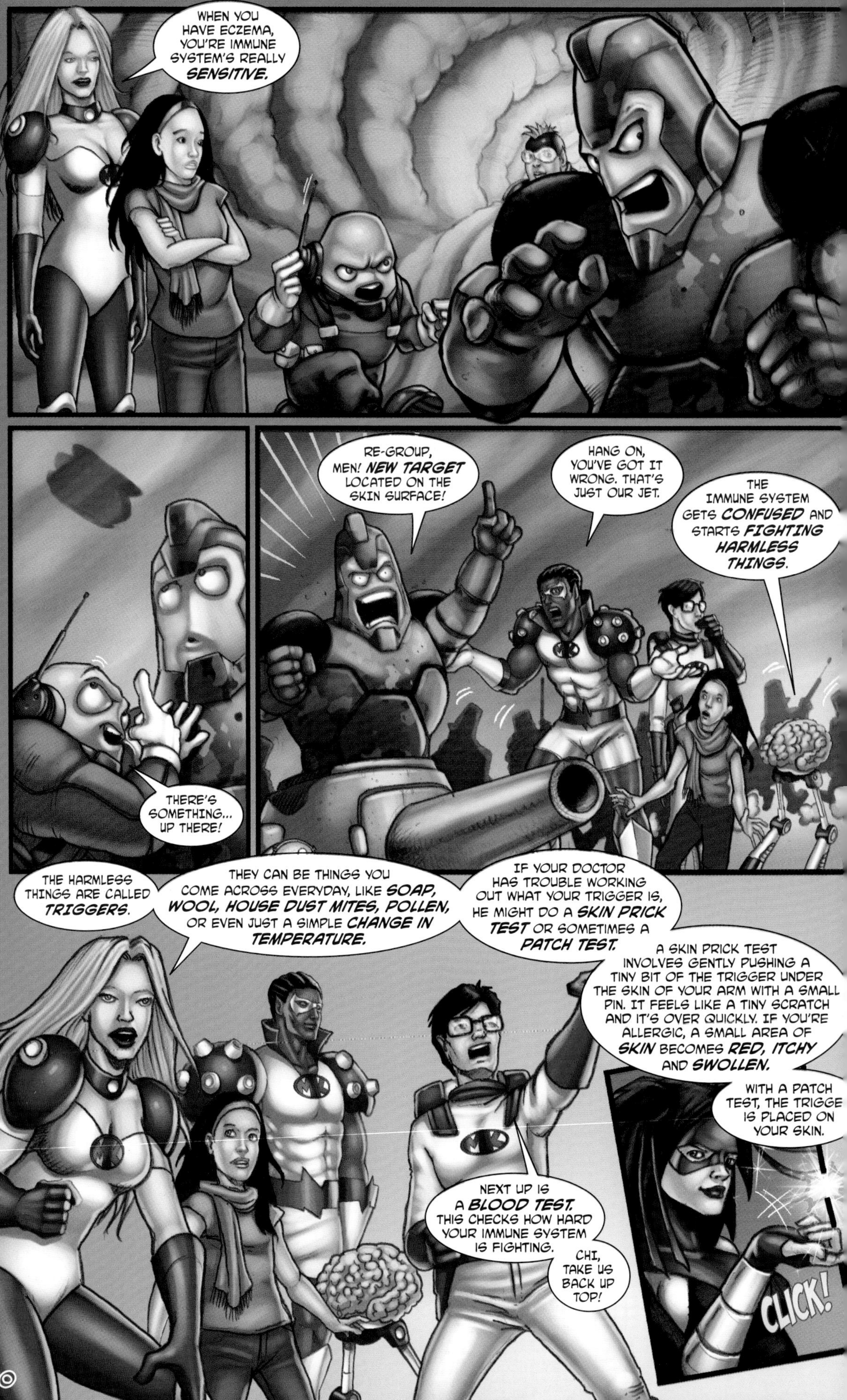

WHEN YOU HAVE ECZEMA, YOU'RE IMMUNE SYSTEM'S REALLY SENSITIVE.
RE-GROUP, MEN! NEW TARGET LOCATED ON THE SKIN SURFACE!
HANG ON, YOU'VE GOT IT WRONG. THAT'S JUST OUR JET.
THE IMMUNE SYSTEM GETS CONFUSED AND STARTS FIGHTING HARMLESS THINGS.
THERE'S SOMETHING... UP THERE!
THE HARMLESS THINGS ARE CALLED TRIGGERS.
THEY CAN BE THINGS YOU COME ACROSS EVERYDAY, LIKE SOAP, WOOL, HOUSE DUST MITES, POLLEN, OR EVEN JUST A SIMPLE CHANGE IN TEMPERATURE.
IF YOUR DOCTOR HAS TROUBLE WORKING OUT WHAT YOUR TRIGGER IS, HE MIGHT DO A SKIN PRICK TEST OR SOMETIMES A PATCH TEST.
A SKIN PRICK TEST INVOLVES GENTLY PUSHING A TINY BIT OF THE TRIGGER UNDER THE SKIN OF YOUR ARM WITH A SMALL PIN. IT FEELS LIKE A TINY SCRATCH AND IT'S OVER QUICKLY. IF YOU'RE ALLERGIC, A SMALL AREA OF SKIN BECOMES RED, ITCHY AND SWOLLEN.
WITH A PATCH TEST, THE TRIGGE IS PLACED ON YOUR SKIN.
NEXT UP IS A BLOOD TEST. THIS CHECKS HOW HARD YOUR IMMUNE SYSTEM IS FIGHTING.
CHI, TAKE US BACK UP TOP!
CLICK!

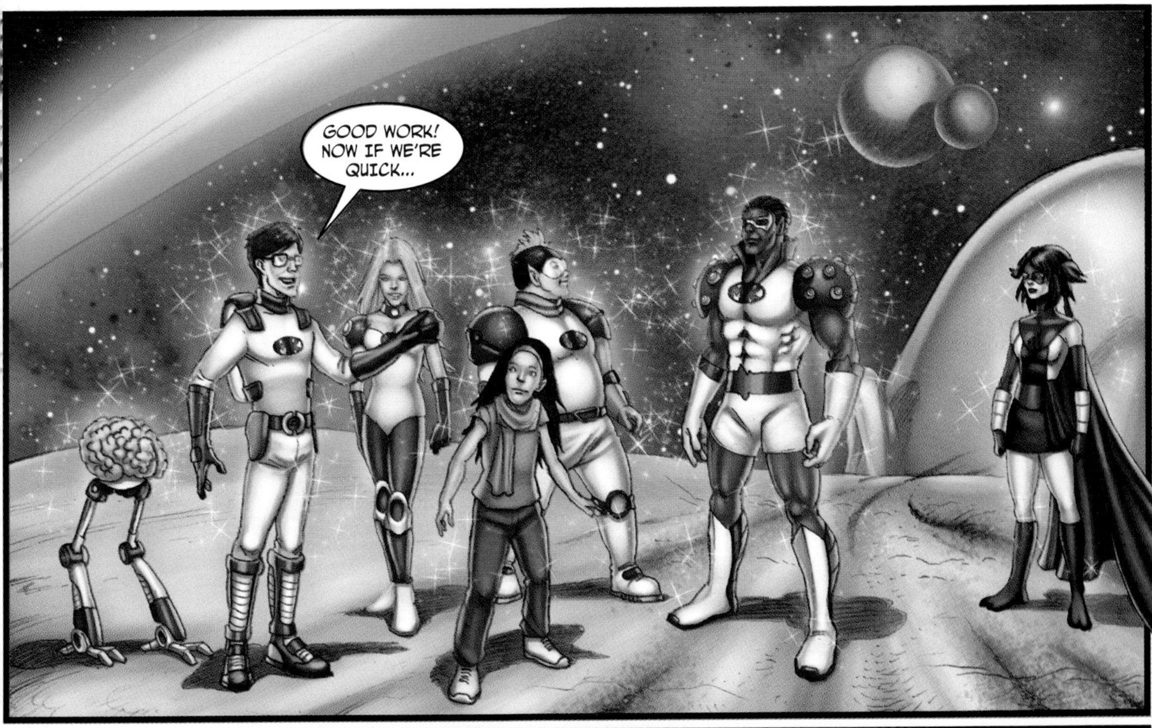
GOOD WORK! NOW IF WE'RE QUICK...

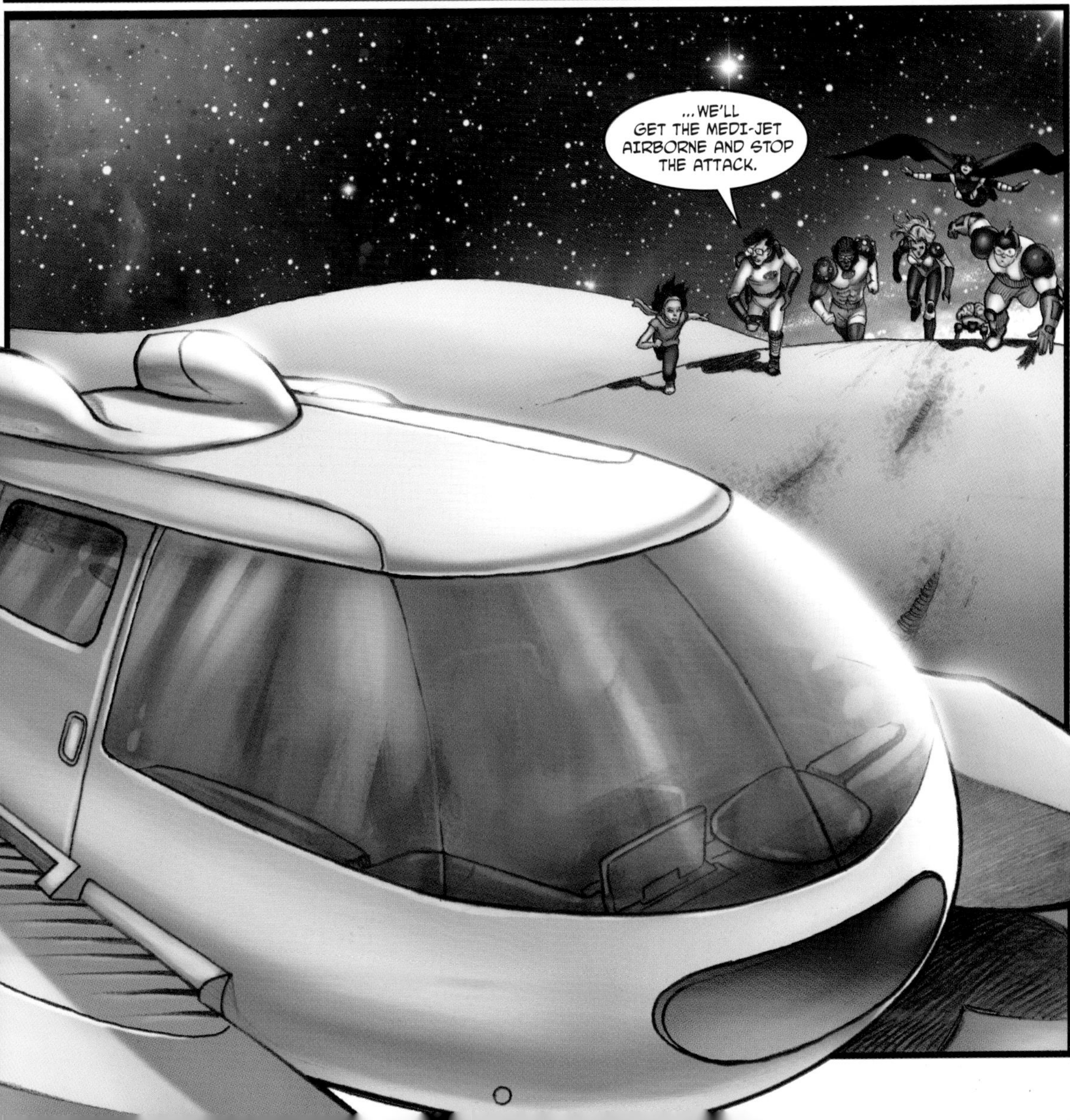
...WE'LL GET THE MEDI-JET AIRBORNE AND STOP THE ATTACK.

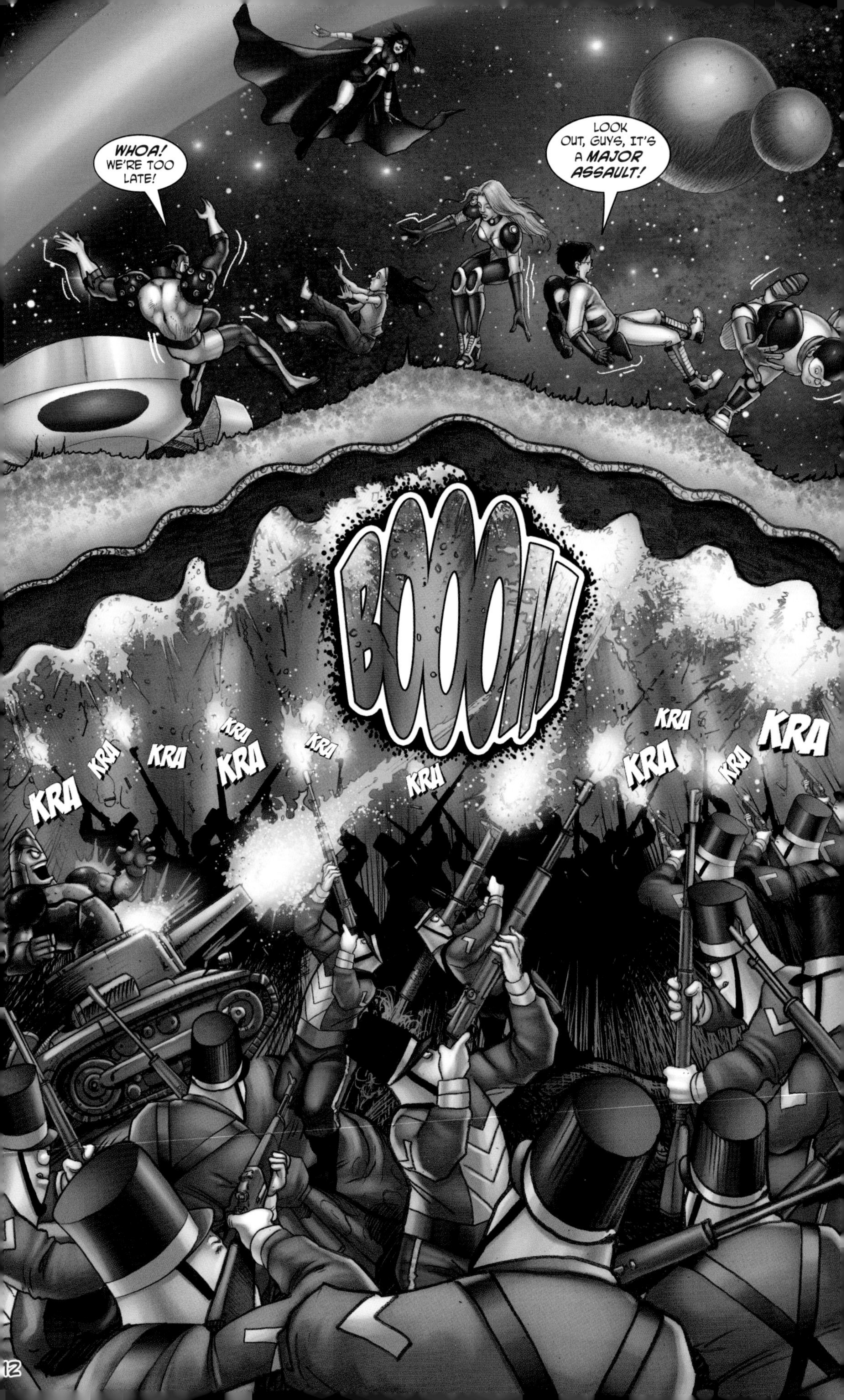
WHOA! WE'RE TOO LATE!
LOOK OUT, GUYS, IT'S A MAJOR ASSAULT!
BOOOM
KRA
KRA
KRA
KRA
KRA
KRA
KRA
KRA
KRA
KRA
KRA
KRA

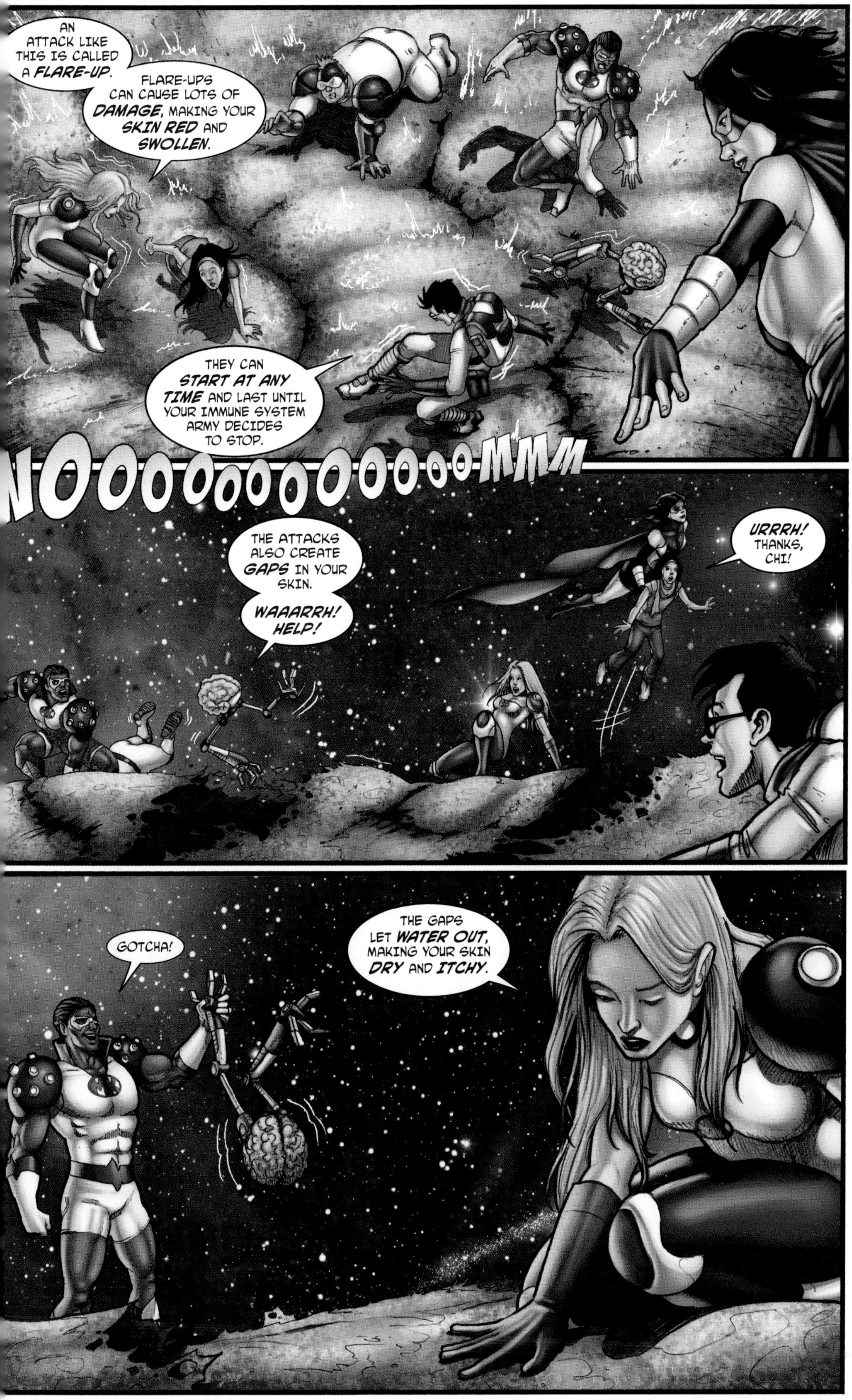
AN ATTACK LIKE THIS IS CALLED A FLARE-UP.
FLARE-UPS CAN CAUSE LOTS OF DAMAGE, MAKING YOUR SKIN RED AND SWOLLEN.
THEY CAN START AT ANY TIME AND LAST UNTIL YOUR IMMUNE SYSTEM ARMY DECIDES TO STOP.
NOOOOOOOOOOOOOMMM
THE ATTACKS ALSO CREATE GAPS IN YOUR SKIN.
WAAARRH! HELP!
URRRH! THANKS, CHI!
GOTCHA!
THE GAPS LET WATER OUT, MAKING YOUR SKIN DRY AND ITCHY.

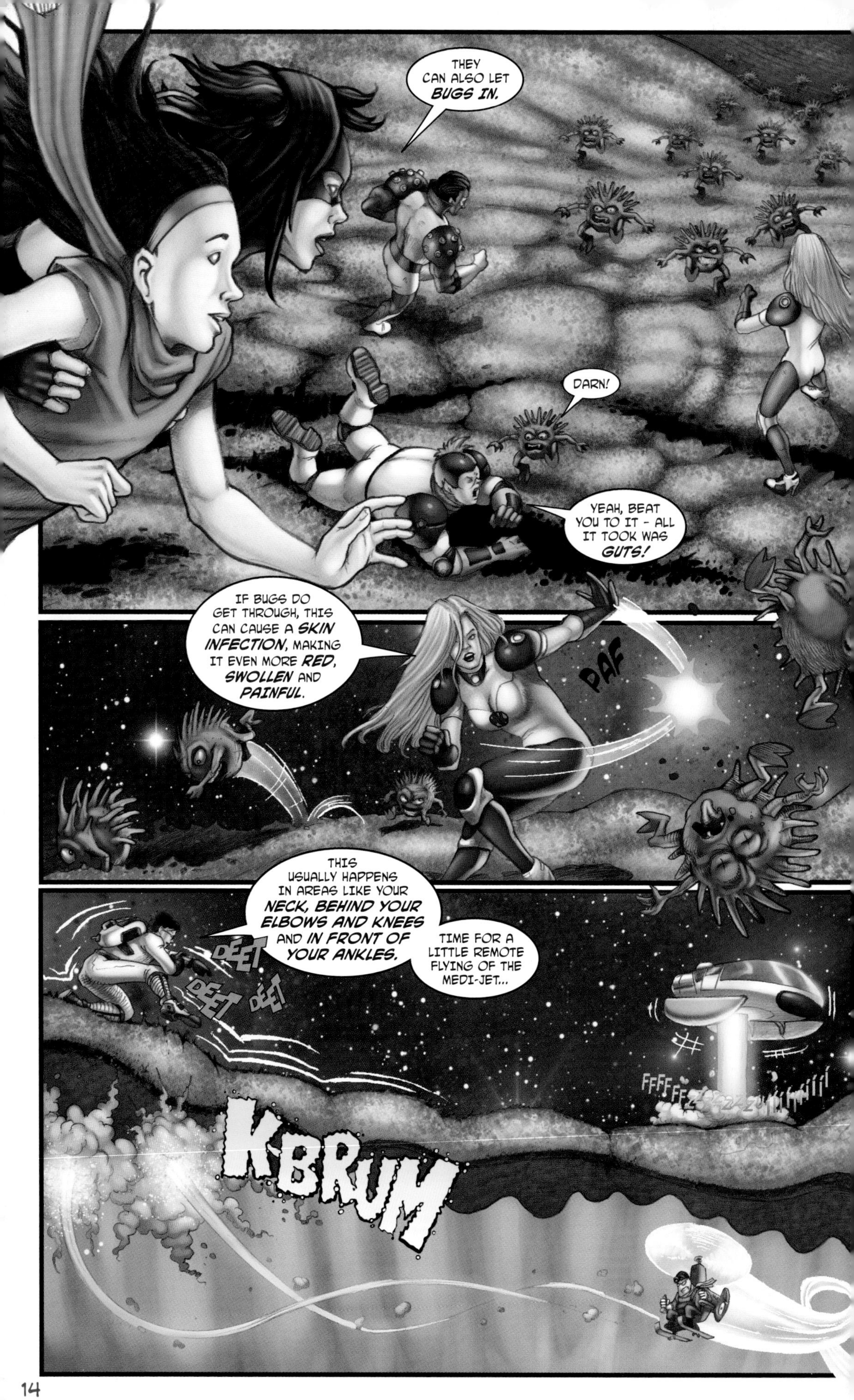

THEY CAN ALSO LET BUGS IN.
DARN!
YEAH, BEAT YOU TO IT - ALL IT TOOK WAS GUTS!
IF BUGS DO GET THROUGH, THIS CAN CAUSE A SKIN INFECTION, MAKING IT EVEN MORE RED, SWOLLEN AND PAINFUL.
PAF
THIS USUALLY HAPPENS IN AREAS LIKE YOUR NECK, BEHIND YOUR ELBOWS AND KNEES AND IN FRONT OF YOUR ANKLES.
DEET
DEET
DEET
TIME FOR A LITTLE REMOTE FLYING OF THE MEDI-JET...
KBRUM

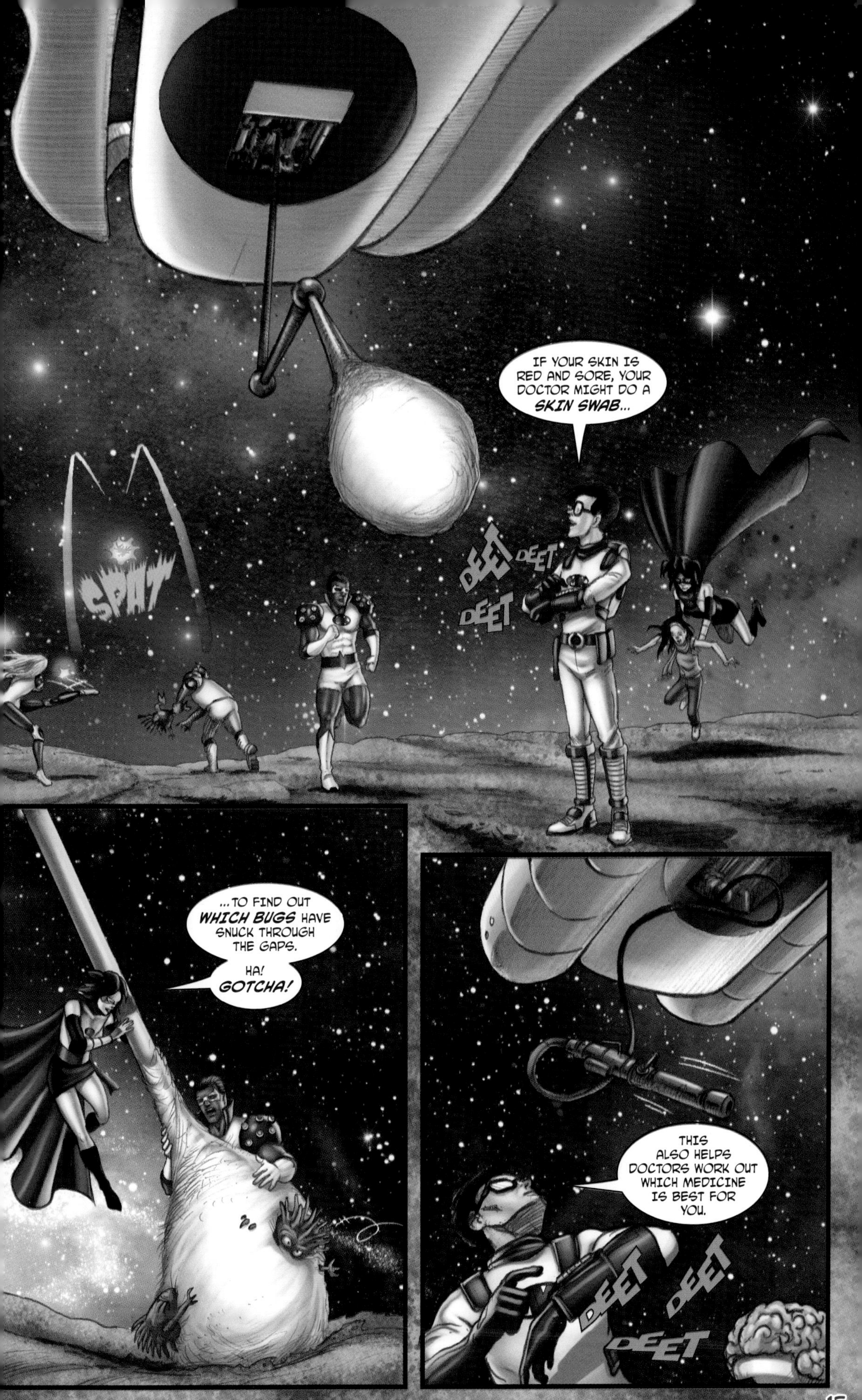
IF YOUR SKIN IS RED AND SORE, YOUR DOCTOR MIGHT DO A SKIN SWAB...
SPAT
DEET
DEET
DEET
...TO FIND OUT WHICH BUGS HAVE SNUCK THROUGH THE GAPS.
HA! GOTCHA!
THIS ALSO HELPS DOCTORS WORK OUT WHICH MEDICINE IS BEST FOR YOU.
DEET
DEET
DEET

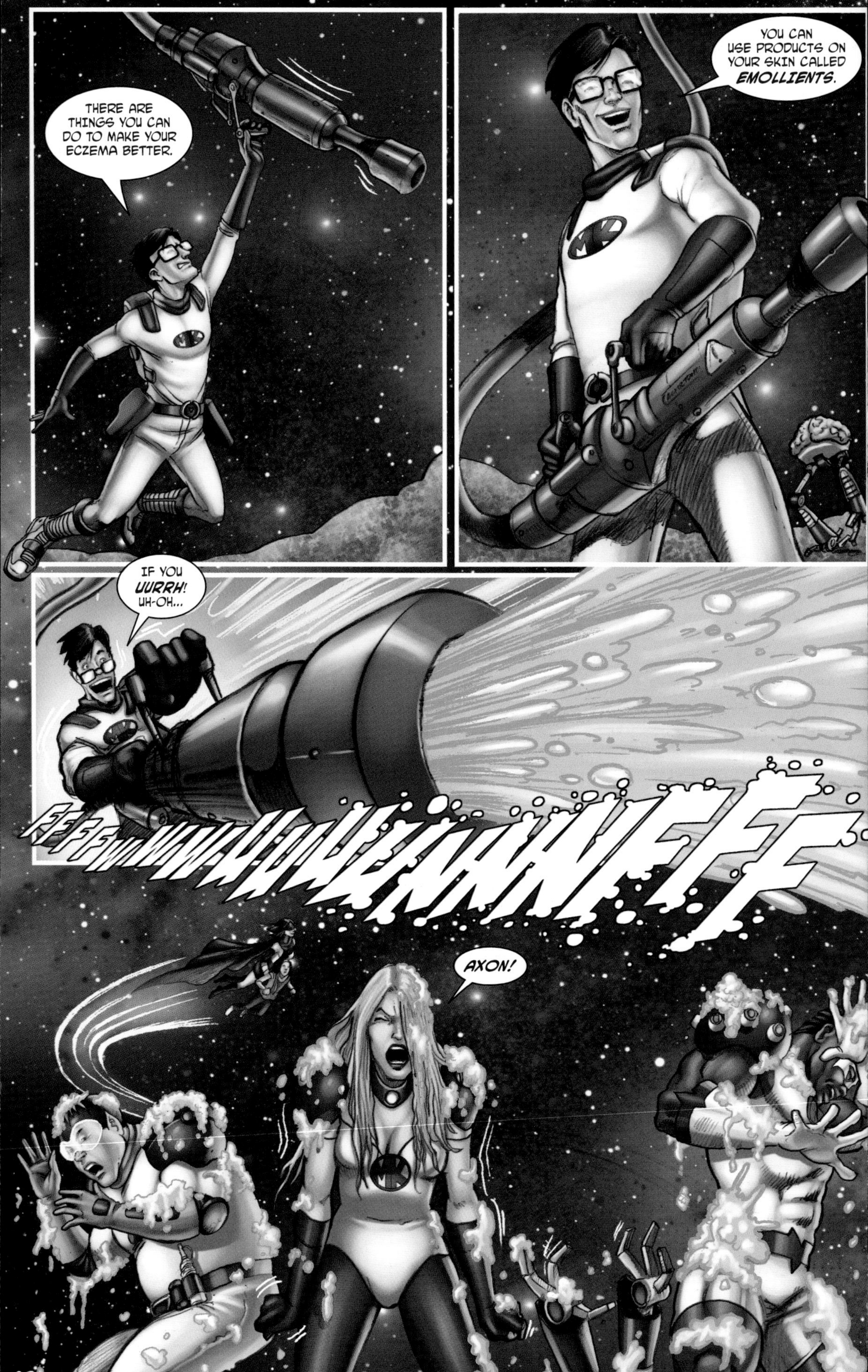
THERE ARE THINGS YOU CAN DO TO MAKE YOUR ECZEMA BETTER.
YOU CAN USE PRODUCTS ON YOUR SKIN CALLED **EMOLLIENTS**.
IF YOU **UURRH!** UH-OH...
FFFFWMMWWUUUUEAAAHNFFFF
AXON!

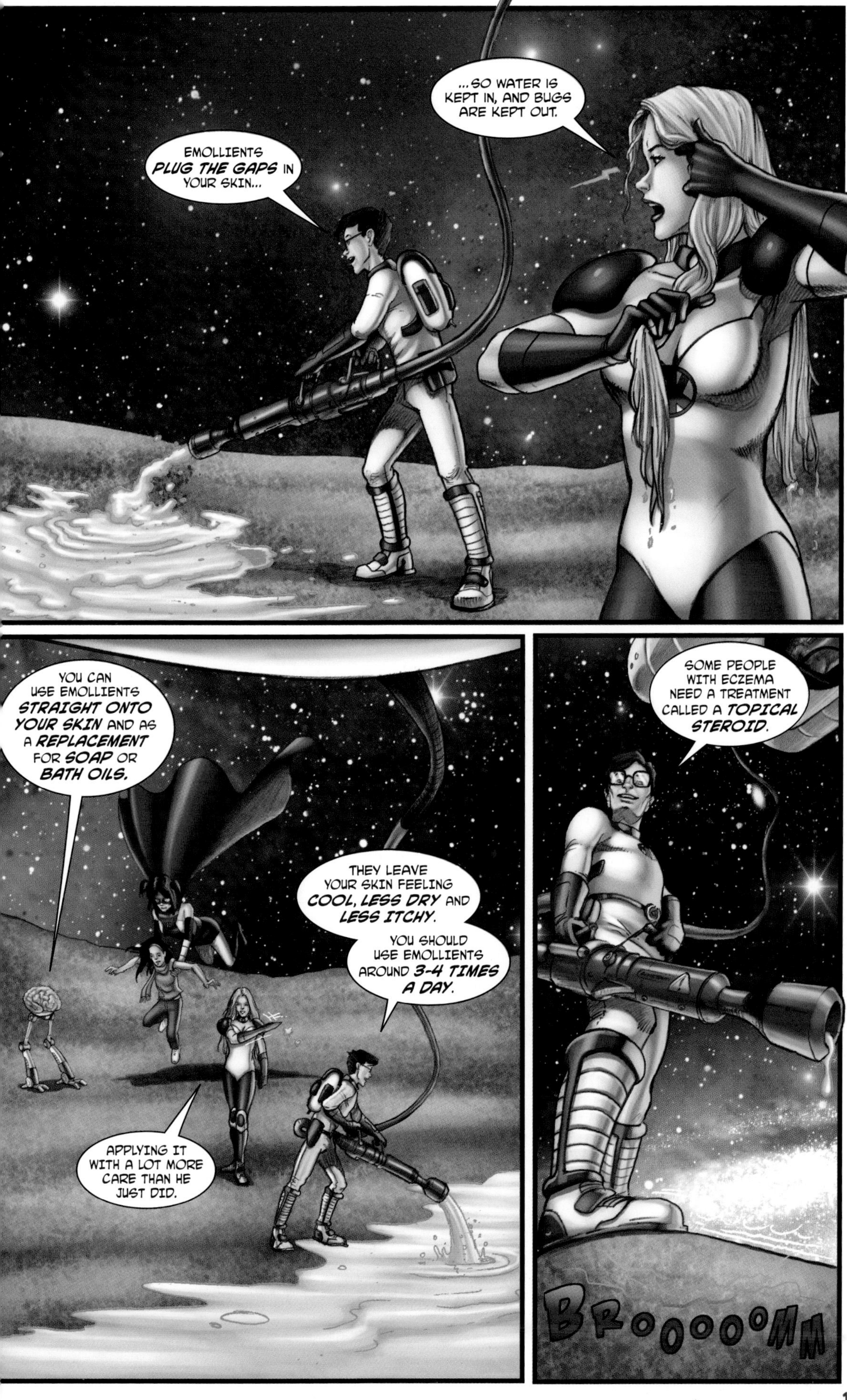
EMOLLIENTS *PLUG THE GAPS* IN YOUR SKIN...
...SO WATER IS KEPT IN, AND BUGS ARE KEPT OUT.
YOU CAN USE EMOLLIENTS *STRAIGHT ONTO YOUR SKIN* AND AS A *REPLACEMENT* FOR *SOAP* OR *BATH OILS.*
THEY LEAVE YOUR SKIN FEELING *COOL, LESS DRY* AND *LESS ITCHY.*
YOU SHOULD USE EMOLLIENTS AROUND *3-4 TIMES A DAY.*
APPLYING IT WITH A LOT MORE CARE THAN HE JUST DID.
SOME PEOPLE WITH ECZEMA NEED A TREATMENT CALLED A *TOPICAL STEROID.*
BROOOOOMM

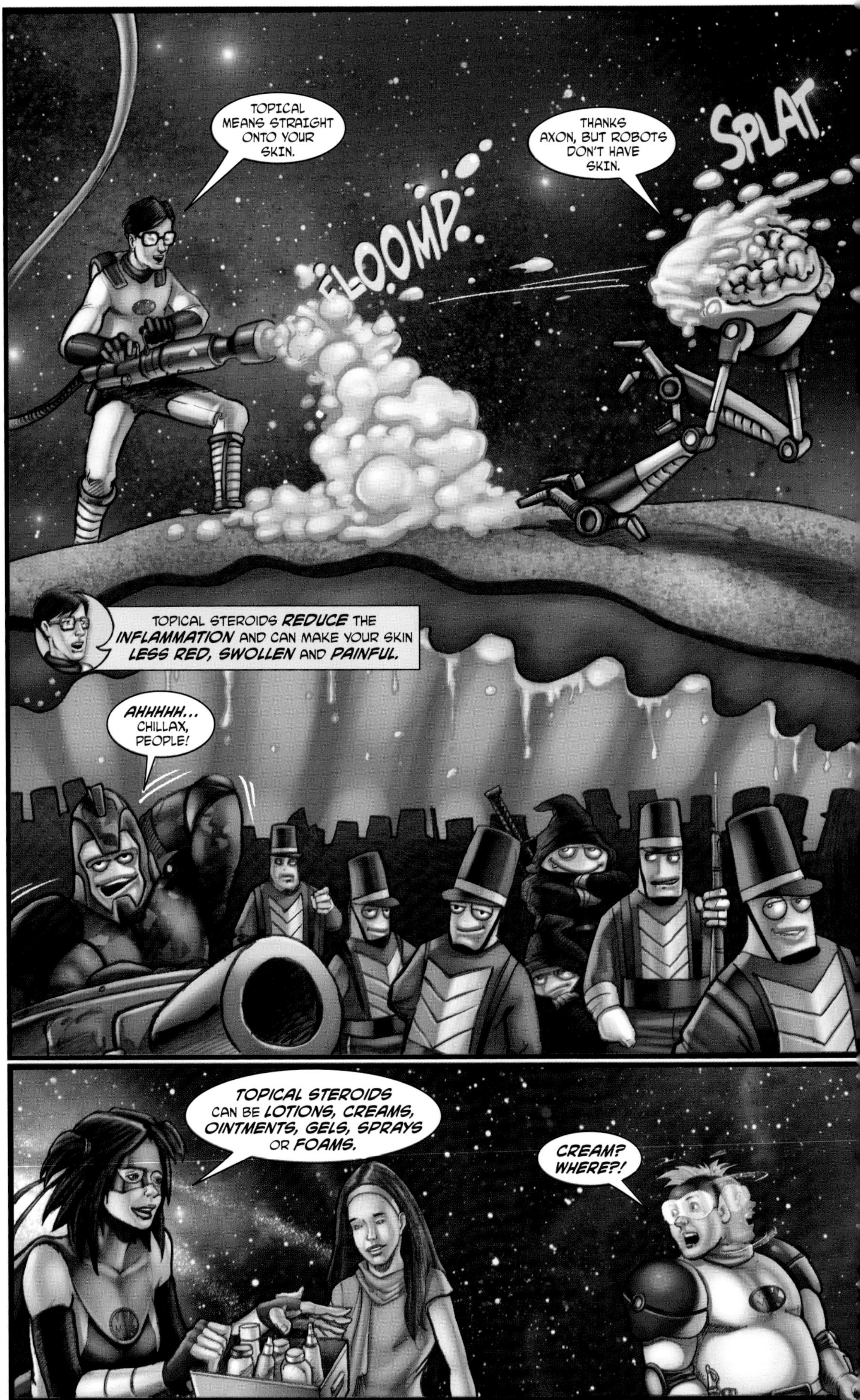
TOPICAL MEANS STRAIGHT ONTO YOUR SKIN.
FLOOMP
THANKS AXON, BUT ROBOTS DON'T HAVE SKIN.
SPLAT
TOPICAL STEROIDS **REDUCE** THE **INFLAMMATION** AND CAN MAKE YOUR SKIN **LESS RED, SWOLLEN** AND **PAINFUL.**
AHHHHH... CHILLAX, PEOPLE!
TOPICAL STEROIDS CAN BE LOTIONS, CREAMS, OINTMENTS, GELS, SPRAYS OR FOAMS.
CREAM? WHERE?!

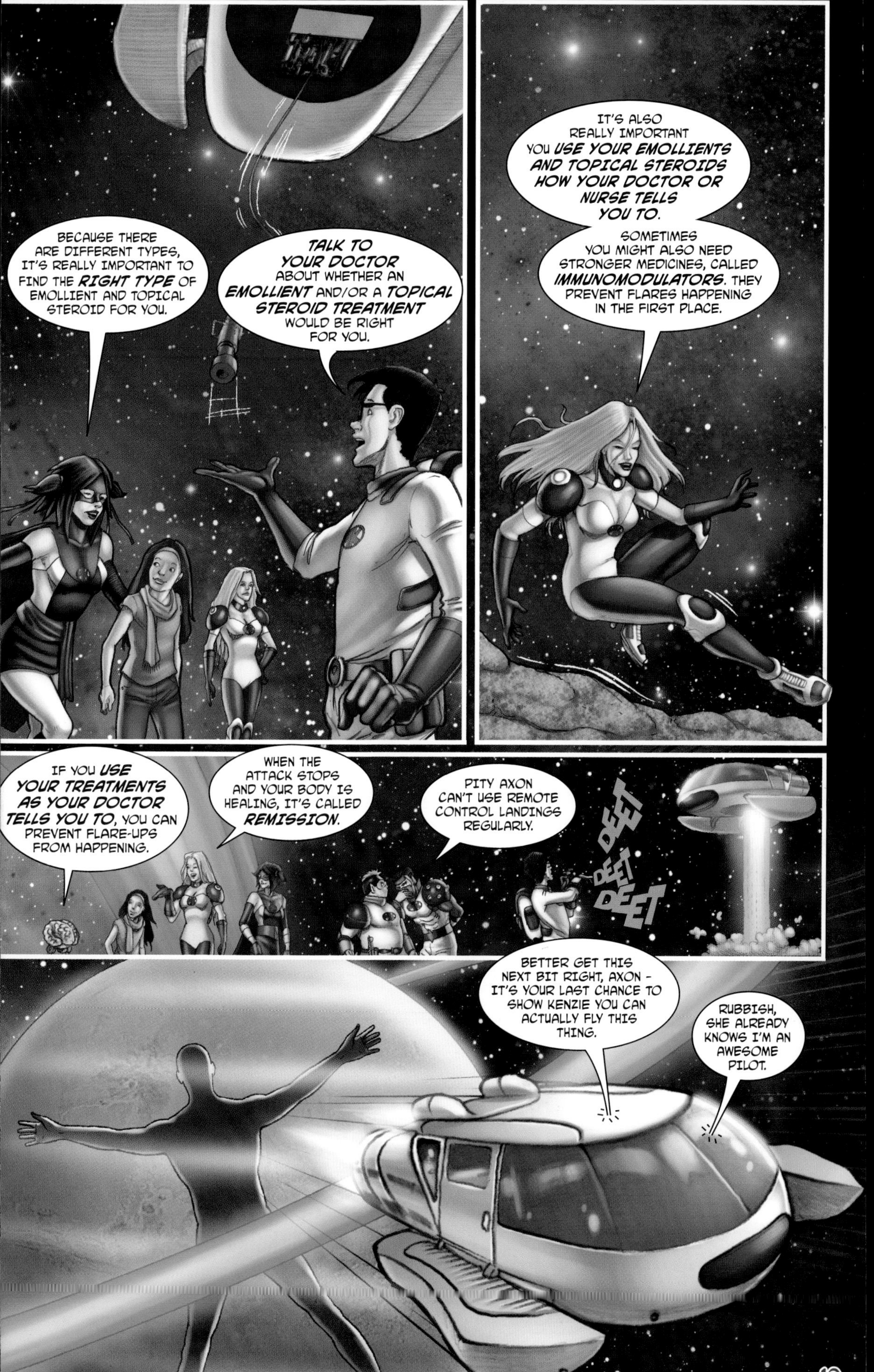
BECAUSE THERE ARE DIFFERENT TYPES, IT'S REALLY IMPORTANT TO FIND THE RIGHT TYPE OF EMOLLIENT AND TOPICAL STEROID FOR YOU.
TALK TO YOUR DOCTOR ABOUT WHETHER AN EMOLLIENT AND/OR A TOPICAL STEROID TREATMENT WOULD BE RIGHT FOR YOU.
IT'S ALSO REALLY IMPORTANT YOU USE YOUR EMOLLIENTS AND TOPICAL STEROIDS HOW YOUR DOCTOR OR NURSE TELLS YOU TO.
SOMETIMES YOU MIGHT ALSO NEED STRONGER MEDICINES, CALLED IMMUNOMODULATORS. THEY PREVENT FLARES HAPPENING IN THE FIRST PLACE.
IF YOU USE YOUR TREATMENTS AS YOUR DOCTOR TELLS YOU TO, YOU CAN PREVENT FLARE-UPS FROM HAPPENING.
WHEN THE ATTACK STOPS AND YOUR BODY IS HEALING, IT'S CALLED REMISSION.
PITY AXON CAN'T USE REMOTE CONTROL LANDINGS REGULARLY.
DEET DEET DEET
BETTER GET THIS NEXT BIT RIGHT, AXON - IT'S YOUR LAST CHANCE TO SHOW KENZIE YOU CAN ACTUALLY FLY THIS THING.
RUBBISH, SHE ALREADY KNOWS I'M AN AWESOME PILOT.

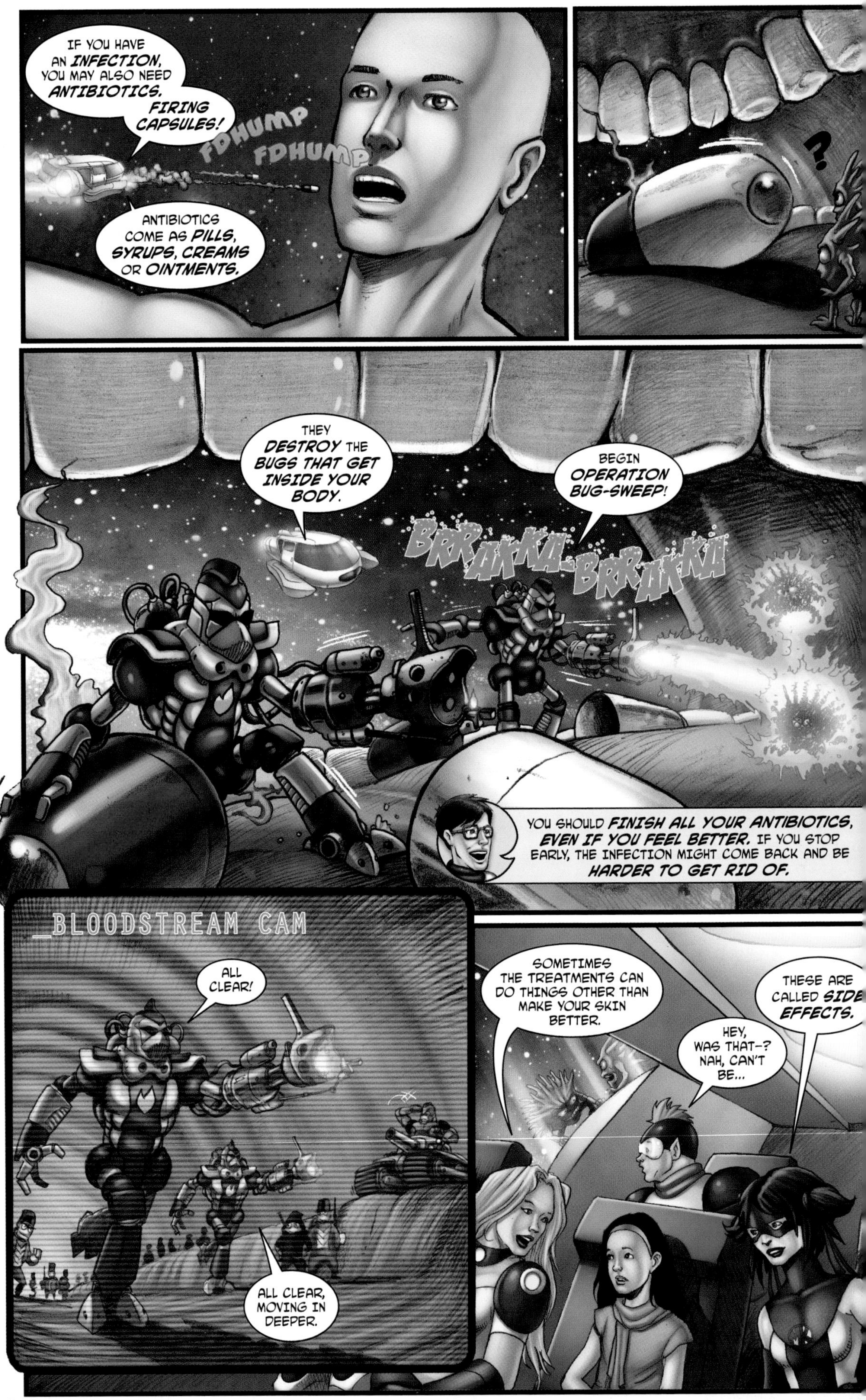

IF YOU HAVE AN INFECTION, YOU MAY ALSO NEED ANTIBIOTICS.
FIRING CAPSULES!
FDHUMP
FDHUMP
ANTIBIOTICS COME AS PILLS, SYRUPS, CREAMS OR OINTMENTS.
?
THEY DESTROY THE BUGS THAT GET INSIDE YOUR BODY.
BEGIN OPERATION BUG-SWEEP!
BRRAKKA-BRRAKKA
YOU SHOULD FINISH ALL YOUR ANTIBIOTICS, EVEN IF YOU FEEL BETTER. IF YOU STOP EARLY, THE INFECTION MIGHT COME BACK AND BE HARDER TO GET RID OF.
_BLOODSTREAM CAM
ALL CLEAR!
ALL CLEAR, MOVING IN DEEPER.
SOMETIMES THE TREATMENTS CAN DO THINGS OTHER THAN MAKE YOUR SKIN BETTER.
THESE ARE CALLED SIDE EFFECTS.
HEY, WAS THAT-? NAH, CAN'T BE...

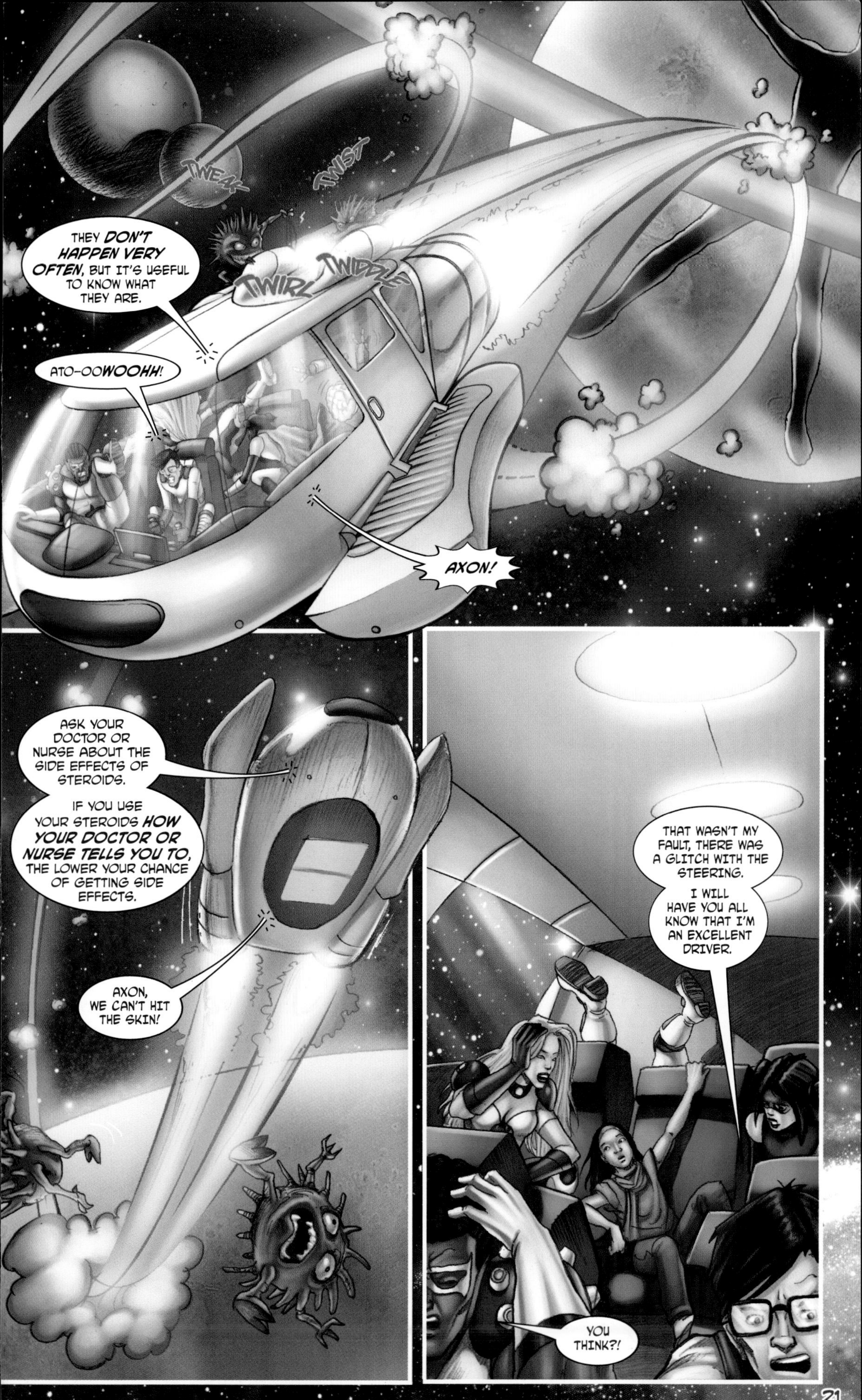
TWEAK
TWIST
THEY **DON'T HAPPEN VERY OFTEN**, BUT IT'S USEFUL TO KNOW WHAT THEY ARE.
TWIRL
TWIDDLE
ATO-OO**WOOHH**!
AXON!
ASK YOUR DOCTOR OR NURSE ABOUT THE SIDE EFFECTS OF STEROIDS.
IF YOU USE YOUR STEROIDS **HOW YOUR DOCTOR OR NURSE TELLS YOU TO**, THE LOWER YOUR CHANCE OF GETTING SIDE EFFECTS.
AXON, WE CAN'T HIT THE SKIN!
THAT WASN'T MY FAULT, THERE WAS A GLITCH WITH THE STEERING.
I WILL HAVE YOU ALL KNOW THAT I'M AN EXCELLENT DRIVER.
YOU THINK?!

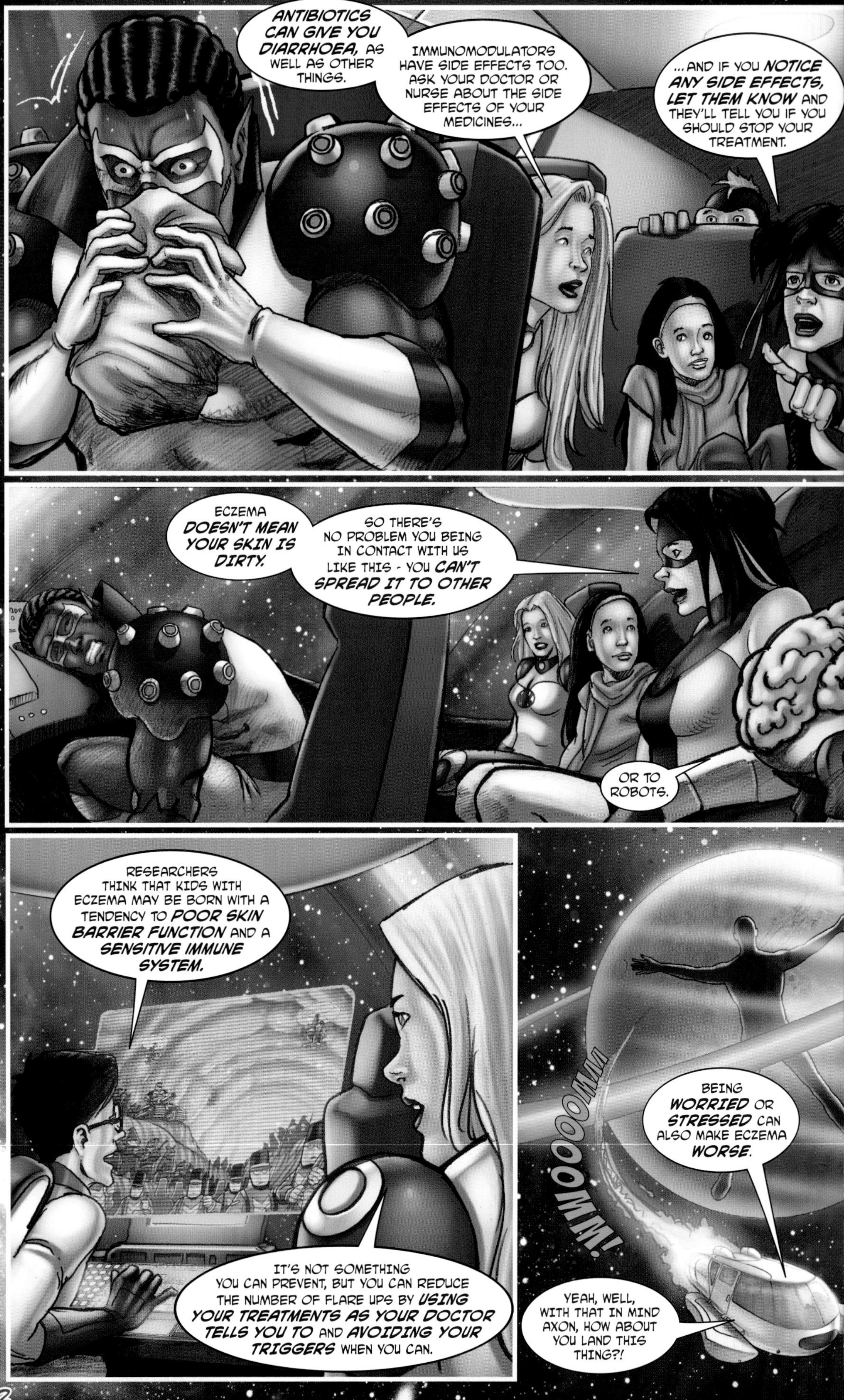
ANTIBIOTICS CAN GIVE YOU DIARRHOEA, AS WELL AS OTHER THINGS.
IMMUNOMODULATORS HAVE SIDE EFFECTS TOO. ASK YOUR DOCTOR OR NURSE ABOUT THE SIDE EFFECTS OF YOUR MEDICINES...
...AND IF YOU NOTICE ANY SIDE EFFECTS, LET THEM KNOW AND THEY'LL TELL YOU IF YOU SHOULD STOP YOUR TREATMENT.
ECZEMA DOESN'T MEAN YOUR SKIN IS DIRTY.
SO THERE'S NO PROBLEM YOU BEING IN CONTACT WITH US LIKE THIS - YOU CAN'T SPREAD IT TO OTHER PEOPLE.
OR TO ROBOTS.
RESEARCHERS THINK THAT KIDS WITH ECZEMA MAY BE BORN WITH A TENDENCY TO POOR SKIN BARRIER FUNCTION AND A SENSITIVE IMMUNE SYSTEM.
IT'S NOT SOMETHING YOU CAN PREVENT, BUT YOU CAN REDUCE THE NUMBER OF FLARE UPS BY USING YOUR TREATMENTS AS YOUR DOCTOR TELLS YOU TO AND AVOIDING YOUR TRIGGERS WHEN YOU CAN.
VVOOOOOMM!
BEING WORRIED OR STRESSED CAN ALSO MAKE ECZEMA WORSE.
YEAH, WELL, WITH THAT IN MIND AXON, HOW ABOUT YOU LAND THIS THING?!

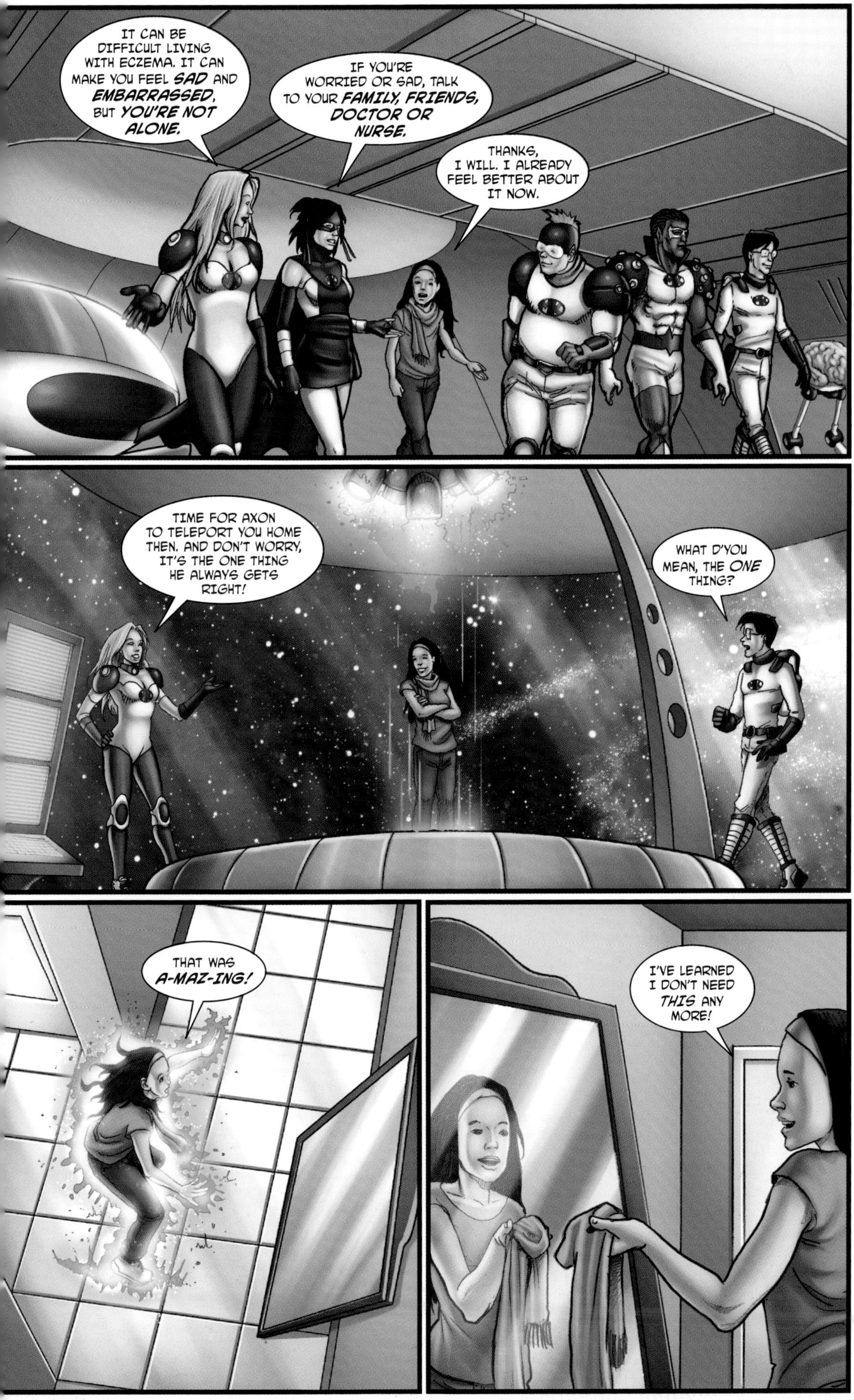
IT CAN BE DIFFICULT LIVING WITH ECZEMA. IT CAN MAKE YOU FEEL SAD AND EMBARRASSED, BUT YOU'RE NOT ALONE.
IF YOU'RE WORRIED OR SAD, TALK TO YOUR FAMILY, FRIENDS, DOCTOR OR NURSE.
THANKS, I WILL. I ALREADY FEEL BETTER ABOUT IT NOW.
TIME FOR AXON TO TELEPORT YOU HOME THEN. AND DON'T WORRY, IT'S THE ONE THING HE ALWAYS GETS RIGHT!
WHAT D'YOU MEAN, THE ONE THING?
THAT WAS A-MAZ-ING!
I'VE LEARNED I DON'T NEED THIS ANY MORE!

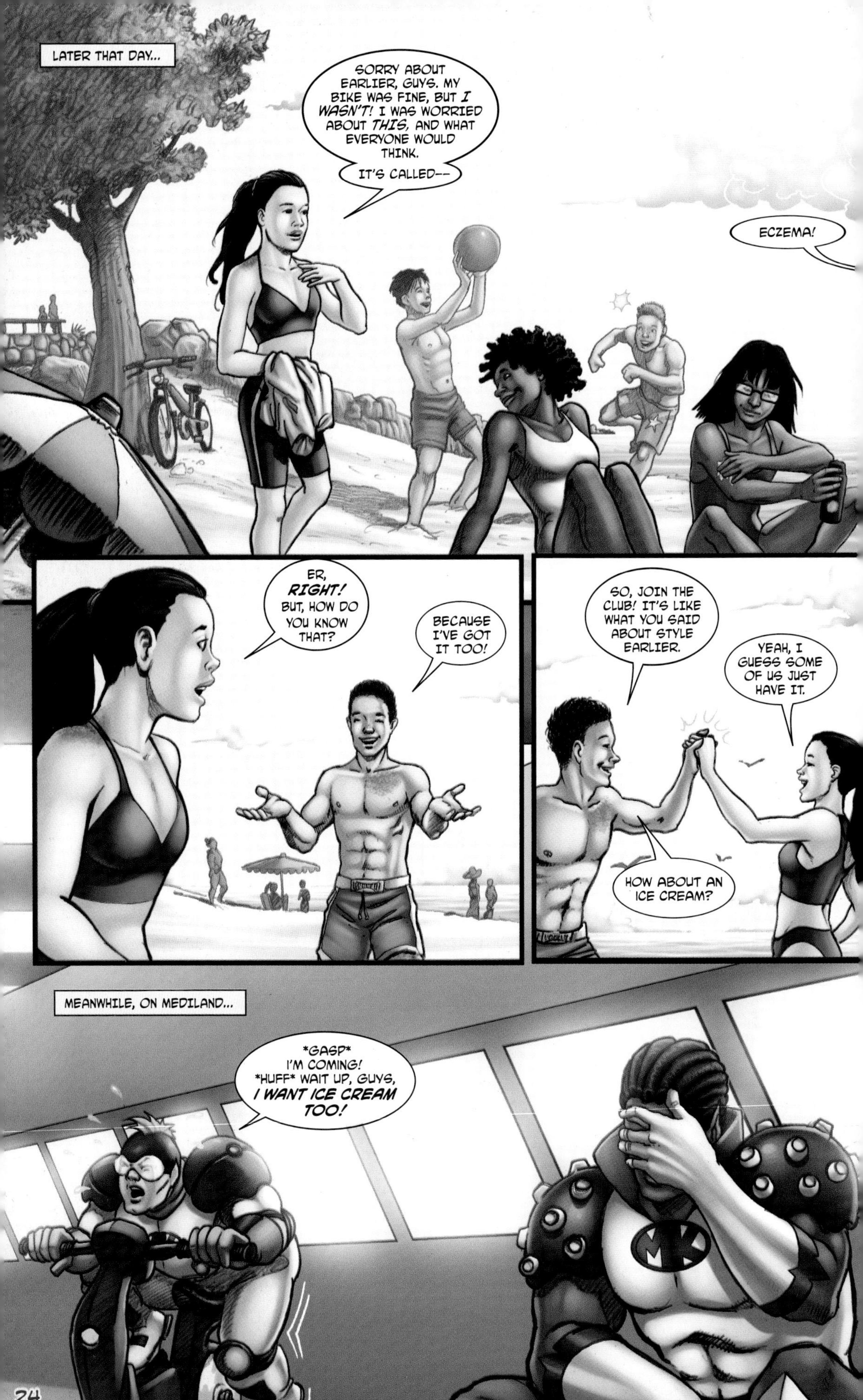
LATER THAT DAY...
SORRY ABOUT EARLIER, GUYS. MY BIKE WAS FINE, BUT I WASN'T! I WAS WORRIED ABOUT THIS, AND WHAT EVERYONE WOULD THINK.
IT'S CALLED--
ECZEMA!
ER, RIGHT! BUT, HOW DO YOU KNOW THAT?
BECAUSE I'VE GOT IT TOO!
SO, JOIN THE CLUB! IT'S LIKE WHAT YOU SAID ABOUT STYLE EARLIER.
YEAH, I GUESS SOME OF US JUST HAVE IT.
HOW ABOUT AN ICE CREAM?
MEANWHILE, ON MEDILAND...
GASP I'M COMING! *HUFF* WAIT UP, GUYS, I WANT ICE CREAM TOO!